THE BEST OF
BROCHURE
DESIGN

07

WILSON HARVEY: LONDON

ROCKPORT

CORPORATE BROCHURES

ANNUAL REPORTS

PRODUCT AND SERVICE BROCHURES

NON-PROFIT, EDUCATIONAL, INSTITUTIONAL, AND HEALTHCARE BROCHURES

SELF-PROMOTIONAL BROCHURES

ARTS, ENTERTAINMENT, AND EVENT BROCHURES

GLOUCESTER MASSACHUSETTS

ROCKPORT
PUBLISHERS

THE BEST OF
BROCHURE
DESIGN 07

WILSON HARVEY: LONDON

© 2003 BY ROCKPORT PUBLISHERS, INC.

FIRST PUBLISHED IN PAPERBACK IN 2004.

ALL RIGHTS RESERVED. NO PART OF THIS BOOK MAY BE
REPRODUCED IN ANY FORM WITHOUT WRITTEN PERMISSION
OF THE COPYRIGHT OWNERS. ALL IMAGES IN THIS BOOK HAVE
BEEN REPRODUCED WITH THE KNOWLEDGE AND PRIOR CON-
SENT OF THE ARTISTS CONCERNED, AND NO RESPONSIBILITY
IS ACCEPTED BY PRODUCER, PUBLISHER, OR PRINTER FOR
ANY INFRINGEMENT OF COPYRIGHT OR OTHERWISE, ARISING
FROM THE CONTENTS OF THIS PUBLICATION. EVERY EFFORT
HAS BEEN MADE TO ENSURE THAT CREDITS ACCURATELY
COMPLY WITH INFORMATION SUPPLIED.

FIRST PUBLISHED IN THE UNITED STATES OF AMERICA BY
ROCKPORT PUBLISHERS, INC. 33 COMMERCIAL STREET
GLOUCESTER, MASSACHUSETTS 01930-5089. TELEPHONE:
(978) 282-9590. FAX (978) 283-2742. WWW.ROCKPUB.COM

ISBN 1-59253-085-0

10 9 8 7 6 5 4 3 2 1

DESIGNED AT WILSON HARVEY. LONDON [+44 (0)20 7420 7700]

COVER IMAGE: FRANK USHER SPRING 2002 BY APPETITE.

PHOTOGRAPHER: ANDYCAMERON.CO.UK, BY KIND
PERMISSION. PERIVAN WHITE DOVE WWW.PERIVAN.CO.UK

PRINTED IN CHINA.

:07

LINEAGE

CONTENTS

INTRODUCTION

IT IS HARD TO DEFINE EXACTLY WHAT MAKES A REALLY GREAT
BROCHURE, BUT IF THERE IS ONE COMMON THREAD ACROSS ALL THE
WORK IN THIS EXTRAORDINARY REVIEW, IT IS SIMPLY THE PASSION. //
EACH AND EVERY PIECE PRESENTED HERE IS FILLED WITH THE HEART
AND SOUL OF A TRULY PASSIONATE DESIGNER AND PROVIDES AN
INSPIRATION TO EVERYONE WITH AN INTEREST IN DESIGN.

FOR A MOMENT IT LOOKED AS IF BROCHURES WOULD BE WIPED AWAY FOREVER BY THE EXCITEMENT OF THE NEW MEDIA BAND-WAGON. BUT JUDGING BY THE INCREDIBLE QUALITY AND QUANTITY OF WORK WE'VE RECEIVED FOR THIS REVIEW, IT SEEMS WE WERE WRONG—THE BROCHURE IS HERE TO STAY.

SO WHAT IS IT ABOUT BROCHURES THAT'S SO SPECIAL? WHY DEDICATE A WHOLE BOOK TO THEM? BROCHURES HAVE AN INDESCRIBABLE POWER: THEY CAN OPEN DOORS, THEY CAN PERSUADE, THEY CAN SELL. A BROCHURE CAN TELL A STORY FOR YOU, IT CAN CHANGE PERCEPTIONS, IT CAN EVEN LIE FOR YOU. IT IS AN EXTREMELY VALUABLE ASSET AND, WHEN USED CORRECTLY, CAN BE A POWERFUL COMMUNICATION TOOL.

BUT WHAT MAKES A GOOD BROCHURE? AND WHAT MAKES A BAD ONE? DESIGN PREACHING (MINE AT LEAST) FOCUSES ON EXCELLENCE IN TERMS OF COMMUNICATION, INFORMATION HANDLING, APPROPRIATENESS, AND EFFECTIVENESS. THIS BOOK IS A REFRESHING LOOK AT WHAT WE AS DESIGNERS BELIEVE IS GOOD AND WHAT THE VISUALLY TRAINED EYE RECOGNIZES AS EXCEPTIONAL WORK. IT IS NOT NECESSARILY WHAT SOLD THE MOST PRODUCTS OR WHAT CREATED THE GREATEST BUZZ IN THE BOARD ROOM. BECAUSE OF THE QUALITY AND CONFIDENCE OF THE WORK, I HAVE LITTLE DOUBT THAT ALL THE WORK SURPASSED CLIENT EXPECTATIONS AND WORKED AS HIGHLY EFFECTIVE MARKETING TOOLS.

DESIGNING AND PRODUCING A BROCHURE IS AN EXTREMELY EMOTIONAL EXPERIENCE—EVERY CLIENT IS DIFFERENT AND EVERY BRIEF HAS ITS OWN CHALLENGES, BUT RECEIVING A BROCHURE SHOULD BE JUST AS EMOTIONAL. THE RECIPIENT SHOULD FEEL TANTALIZED BY THE PIECE, THEY SHOULD WANT TO TURN THE PAGE, THEY SHOULD BE SEDUCED BY IT. THIS BOOK IS A CELEBRATION OF SOME OF THAT WORK—WORK THAT MAKES YOU SIT UP AND TAKE NOTICE, WORK THAT EVOKES A REACTION, GOOD OR BAD, WORK THAT SLAPS YOU ROUND THE FACE, OR WORK THAT IS SIMPLY A CREDIT TO THE CLIENT FOR BREAKING THE MOLD AND LETTING IT HAPPEN.

IN COMPILING THIS VALUABLE RESOURCE, WE'VE TALKED WITH DESIGNERS ALL OVER THE WORLD, ALL WITH ONE COMMON PASSION—GOOD DESIGN. IT IS AN HONOR TO SHARE THEIR PASSION WITH YOU. OUR GRATITUDE GOES TO EVERYONE WHO GENEROUSLY SUBMITTED WORK. I'M ONLY SORRY WE COULDN'T SHOW IT ALL.

PAUL BURGESS AND THE TEAM AT WILSON HARVEY

ARTWORKER:
PETE USHER

DESIGNERS:
PAUL BURGESS
WAI LAU
BEN WOOD
GRAHAM FARR
DAN ELLIOTT

JUDGES:
PAUL BURGESS
DAN ELLIOTT
WAI LAU
GRAHAM FARR
BEN WOOD

ART DIRECTOR:
PAUL BURGESS

CORPORATE BROCHURES

INTERBRAND // PINKHAUS // RADFORD WALLIS // KO CRÉATION // HAND MADE GROUP //
SALTERBAXTER // EMERY VINCENT DESIGN // LAVA GRAPHIC DESIGNERS // POULIN + MORRIS //
FORM // ROSE DESIGN ASSOCIATES // ATTIK // HORNALL ANDERSON DESIGN WORKS //
GRAPHICULTURE // DESIGN ASYLUM // NB:STUDIO // FABIO ONGARATO DESIGN //
CAMPAÑEROS // THIRTEEN DESIGN // BOSTOCK & POLLITT

:01

Breaking boundaries:
Business law for
the real world

2002

Highway 407
Toronto Canada

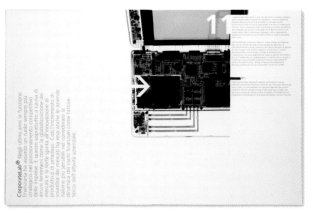

ART DIRECTOR:
INTERBRAND

DESIGNER:
ZOE SCUTTS

PHOTOGRAPHER:
INTERBRAND

CLIENT:
UNICREDIT

SOFTWARE AND
HARDWARE:
PHOTOSHOP
QUARK
MAC G4

PRINTING:
ITALY

UK

>Una nuova banca… Un modo
diverso di guardare i mercati…
Uno sguardo oltre le prime
impressioni…Think again

The power behind
European finance

UBM
UniCredit Banca Mobiliare

001
INTERBRAND
UBM BROCHURE

Soon, most business-to-business commerce will take place in e-marketplaces on the Internet, yet few businesses are able to complete transactions online, even fewer have their business processes integrated, and practically none have an e-business strategy.

Despite these facts, e-business is booming. And if your company plans to be around in the next decade it will be eagerly embracing e-business too. Of course, it's not something you want to do simply because everybody else seems to be doing it.

You want to do e-business because it can give your company a genuine edge.

And that's where Sterling Commerce comes in.

USA

ART DIRECTOR:	DESIGNER:	PRODUCTION	COPYWRITER:	CLIENT:	SOFTWARE AND	MATERIALS:	PRINTING:
CHRISTOPHER VICE	RAELENE MERCER	MANAGER:	FRANK	STERLING	HARDWARE:	MCCOY SILK +	GEORGE RICE &
		SUZANNE	CUNNINGHAM	COMMERCE	QUARKXPRESS	MOHAWK	SONS, CALIFORNIA
		BERNSTEIN			MAC	SUPERFINE	
						SMOOTH	

our knowledge is your edge

When you sell on the Internet, your market is global by definition. That's great, but how do you make it work?

So you saved 18% on 6,000 tons of copper in an online reverse auction. Now what?

Well, your savings are not just limited to finding lower cost goods. The real reason more and more of your purchasing and selling is going to shift to the Internet is that the payback is immediate. Doing business online is a concrete way to lower procurement costs, streamline your supply chain, broaden your selling channels and shorten your time to market.

But all these efficiencies don't just happen automatically. Online transactions have to be linked to outside shippers and financial institutions and to your own internal back-end systems.

ART DIRECTORS:
STUART RADFORD
ANDREW WALLIS

DESIGNERS:
STUART RADFORD
ANDREW WALLIS

PHOTOGRAPHER:
VARIOUS

CLIENT:
REX FEATURES

SOFTWARE:
QUARKXPRESS

MATERIALS:
CAIRN MULTI
BOARD 350GSM
GALERIE SILK
170GSM

PRINTING:
CTD CAPITA

003
RADFORD WALLIS
REX FEATURES

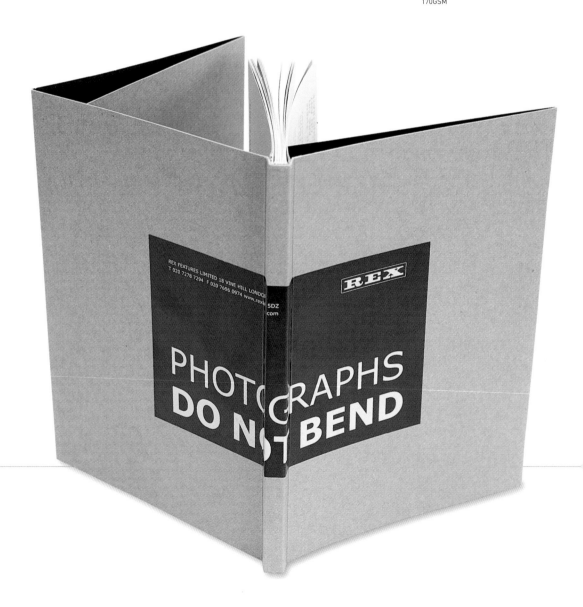

D.D'Aronco & Associés inc._
Ingénieurs-conseils

004
KO CRÉATION
D D'ARONCO & ASSOCIÉS
SELF-PROMO

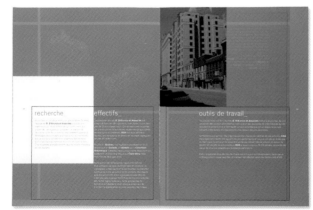

ART DIRECTOR:
KO CRÉATION

DESIGNERS:
ANNIE LACHAPELLE
DENIS DULUDE

CLIENT:
D D'ARONCO &
ASSOCIÉS INC

SOFTWARE:
PHOTOSHOP
QUARKXPRESS

ART DIRECTOR:
ALESSANDRO
ESTERI

DESIGNER:
GIONA MAIARELLI

PHOTOGRAPHER:
ALESSANDRO
ESTERI

CLIENT:
LANIFICIO DEL
CASENTINO

SOFTWARE AND
HARDWARE:
QUARK
MAC

MATERIALS:
FEDRIGONI

PRINTING:
OFFSET

005
HAND MADE GROUP
LANIFICIO DEL CASENTINO
CORPORATE PROFILE

ITALY

Defy convention
Clients don't need to hear why
they can't do something. They
need to be shown how they can.

New perspectives
We never accept things
at face value. If we think
something doesn't make
sense, we question it. If we
believe there's a better way
to do it, we say so. And if
we're right, then we help
you go for it.

Intrigued?

Breaking boundaries
Business law for
the real world

ART DIRECTOR:	DESIGNER:	CLIENT:	SOFTWARE AND	MATERIALS:	PRINTING:
PENNY BAXTER	ANDREA CAREY	TITE & LEWIS	HARDWARE:	MONADNOCK	LITHO
			QUARKXPRESS	ASTROLITE	
			MACINTOSH		

UK

407

99 years

99-year concession period

flexible tolling
Owners have potential flexibility on toll charges, providing significant upside opportunities.

population growth
Passes through some of the fastest growing and most affluent areas of Toronto.

Highway 407 Average Workday Trips

traffic growth
12.6% growth in vehicle kilometres travelled year on year (2001 on 2000).

congested competing route
Runs parallel to Highway 401 — one of the most congested highways in North America, carrying on average 400,000 vehicles per workday at its busiest point.

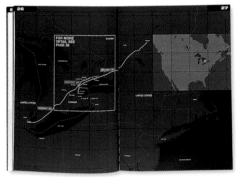

|007

EMERY VINCENT DESIGN
PROSPECTUS 2002

ART DIRECTOR:
EMERY VINCENT
DESIGN

DESIGNER:
EMERY VINCENT
DESIGN

CLIENT:
MACQUARIE
INFRASTRUCTURE
GROUP

407 **The largest toll road privatisation in the world.**

MACQUARIE INFRASTRUCTURE GROUP PROSPECTUS 2002

Highway 407 Toronto Canada

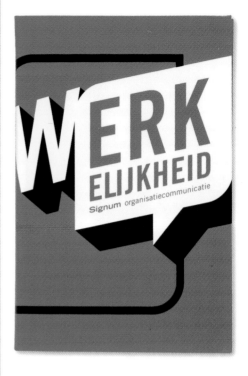

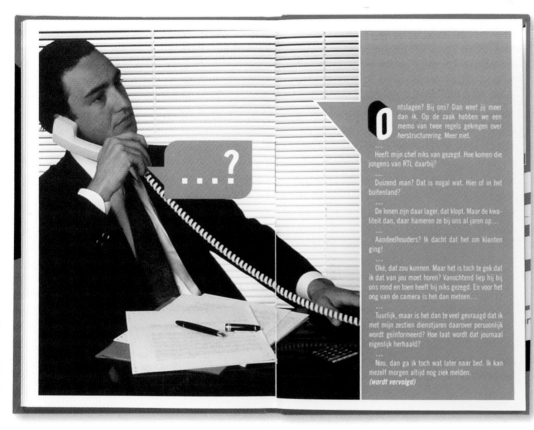

008
LAVA GRAPHIC DESIGNERS
WERKELIJKHEID (REALITY)

ART DIRECTOR:
YKE BARTELS

DESIGNERS:
YKE BARTELS
DAAN JANSSENS

PHOTOGRAPHER:
ROYALTY-FREE
STOCK PHOTOS

CLIENT:
SIGNUM

SOFTWARE AND
HARDWARE:
ILLUSTRATOR
QUARKXPRESS
MAC G4

MATERIALS:
CHRONOLUX

PRINTING:
RIJSER

DUKE CLINIC

Summer 2001

009
POULIN + MORRIS
DUKE CLINIC
COMMEMORATIVE BOOK

DUKE CLINIC

Summer 2001

DETAIL VIEW OF
SOUTH ENTRANCE FROM THE GARDEN

PREVIOUS PAGE
VIEW OF MAIN LOBBY FROM
UPPER BRIDGE LEVEL

VIEW OF BRIDGE LEVEL LOBBY
WITH STAIR AND
ESCALATOR CONNECTIONS TO BELOW

VIEW OF CONNECTING BRIDGE,
LOOKING FROM CLINIC TOWARD
THE GARAGE

ART DIRECTOR:	DESIGNER:	CLIENT:	SOFTWARE:	MATERIALS:	PRINTING:
L. RICHARD POULIN	L. RICHARD POULIN	DUKE UNIVERSITY MEDICAL CENTER	QUARKXPRESS	SAPPI LUSTRO	HUTCHINSON ALLGOOD

USA

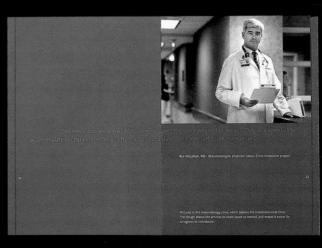

The new clinics are a marked improvement over the space we used to work in. They've allowed us to accommodate our patients better, and from a functional standpoint they just make more sense.

Rex McCallum, MD - Rheumatologist; physician liaison, Clinic renovation project

Pictured in the rheumatology clinic, which adjoins the endocrine/renal clinic. The design allows the services to share space as needed, and makes it easier for caregivers to collaborate.

ART DIRECTORS:
PAULA BENSON
PAUL WEST

DESIGNERS:
TOM CRABTREE
CHRIS HILTON

CLIENT:
MTV

SOFTWARE:
FREEHAND
PHOTOSHOP
QUARKXPRESS

MATERIALS:
PAPER AND BOARD

PRINTING:
FOIL BLOCKED
COVER, 4-COLOR
LITHO + SPOT
VARNISH

UK

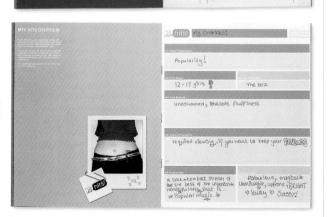

010

FORM
MTV BRAND MANUAL

filtrate **PREZIOSITA'**

perfette **TEXTURE**

Visione attraverso una grata di un interno esotico-coloniale. Penombre e sfumature, luci soffuse, luminosità discreta, riflessi dorati. Aspetti setosi, mescolanze di lucido e opaco, fluidità e leggerezza. Minuscoli armaturati ed intrecci a canestro.

FILTERED PRECIOUSNESS.
View of an exotic-colonial interior through a grid. Semi-darkness and shades, soft lights, discrete brightness, golden hues. Silky appearance, mixture of bright and mat, fluidity and lightness. Tiny weaves and basket weaves.

colori **MATERICI**

Le gamme colore si rifanno ai cromatismi presi da sostanze e materie alquanto inedite.
Gessosi. Colori impuri che richiamano i colori della calce, gesso, stucco, sabbie, pietre.
Cosmetici. Colori delle polveri e creme da make-up Tonalità epidermiche e tocco metallico polverizzato.
Preziosi. Colori scuri, filtrati, ombreggiati. L'oriente nei toni delle penombre: i violacei, i blu, i beige dorati.
Bucolici. Colori olfattivi. Un bouquet di fiori, erbe, piante presi da orti e giardini.
Energetici. Colori forti ispirati dal mondo pubblicitario, dal dinamismo moderno e da folklori latini.

MATERIAL COLOURS.
Colour shades with chromatisms of substances and materials that border on the unusual.
Chalky *The impure colours of lime, chalk, putty, sand, stone*
Cosmetics. *Powder and make-up colours. Skin-deep hues and a powder metal touch*
Precious. *Dark, filtered, shadowy colours. Oriental semi-dark hues: purples, blues, golden beiges*
Bucolic. *Olfactory colours. A bouquet of flowers, herbs, vegetable and flower gardens*
Energetic. *Bright colours inspired by the world of advertising, modern verve and Latin folklore.*

CLASS

seduzione **TATTILE**

E' sicuramente una stagione all'insegna dei piaceri sensoriali dove il tatto acquista sempre più importanza. Le sensazioni più innovative provengono da mischie plurime di fibre: lana/seta/mohair, cotone/lino/lana e dall'uso di prodotti ausiliari inediti come il lattice, il silicone, il Teflon. Inoltre i finissaggi completano il risultato tattile con l'utilizzo di enzimi, sabbiature, lavaggi "stone".

SEDUCTIVE TOUCH.
This is certainly a season under the banner of sensory pleasures where touch becomes increasingly important. The most innovative sensations come from multi-fibre blends such as wool/silk/mohair, cotton/linen/wool and from unexpected auxiliary products such as latex, silicon, Teflon. Enzyme and sandblast finishes, "stone" washing give the final touch.

armonie **BOTANICHE**

Natura vegetale in mostra. Aspetto delavato, tinture organiche. Raffinata semplicità. Freschezza e cromatismi presi da giardini in fiore. Armature semplici come tela, canvas e panama. Disegnature con leggeri riquadri da fazzoletti d'epoca.

BOTANIC HARMONIES.
Natural plant life on display. Washed-out appearance, organic dyes. Refined simplicity. Freshness and shades from blossomed gardens. Simple weaves such as in cloth, canvas and panama. Old-handkerchief patterns with light window panes.

aspetti **ARTIGIANALI**

Imperfezioni volute, superfici irregolari, aspetti granulosi. Rilievi e rugosità con uso di filati grossi alternati a filati sottili. Una nuova rusticità contenuta e raffinata con fondi leggermente crepe.

HANDICRAFT APPEARANCE
Hand-made imperfections, uneven surfaces, grainy effect. Reliefs or roughness obtained with alternating coarse and fine yarns. A new restrained and refined rustic look with slightly crepe backgrounds.

ITALY

ART DIRECTOR:
ALESSANDRO ESTERI

DESIGNER:
GIONA MAIARELLI

CLIENT:
LANIFICIO DEL CASENTINO

SOFTWARE AND HARDWARE:
QUARKXPRESS MAC

MATERIALS:
FEDRIGONI

PRINTING:
OFFSET

Partial left page:

della bellezza e
Tessile
, che si
o, seducono
ficie e levigate, grana
line e compatta
sidratata. Aspetti
, porcellanati,
di filati sottilissimi.

SMOOTHENSS.
beauty and well-
etic textiles.
seductive textiles.
f polished surfaces.
impact fabric grains
drated skin. Silky,
, pearlescent
Use of extra-thin

CI
rivisitati

Basic modernizzato.
Ritorno a tipologie tradizionali
re-interpretate. Disegnature
spesso in bianco e nero ma
con interventi tecnologici.

CLASSICS REVISITED.
Modern basics. Traditional
reinterpretations return. Frequent
black and white motifs with
technological additions.

INTERVISTA/INTERVIEW
Alfio Aldrovandi
DIRETTORE GENERALE DEL LANIFICIO DEL CASENTINO
GENERAL MANAGER OF LANIFICIO DEL CASENTINO

ORE 8 DEL MATTINO:

Il Lanificio si sveglia con il rumore incessante delle sue macchine e già risuonano i passi di Alfio Aldrovandi, che incontriamo davanti al suo primo caffè nero bollente. 47 anni, trent'anni di lavoro nel settore tessile e nove al Lanificio del Casentino da due anni dirige questa azienda con quella imprenditorialie che deriva dalla lunga esperienza maturata sul campo.

A che punto siamo con la produzione, direttore?

Ormai il Lanificio del Casentino si è stabilizzato sulla fascia media e medio-alta di mercato con 2,5 milioni di metri venduti anno. Lei capisce che a questo livello non possiamo permetterci il massimo errore. Quindi lo sforzo maggiore in questo momento è quello di "affinare", in tutti i sensi. Ogni persona che lavora qui dentro deve essere sensibilizzata alla nuova realtà e quindi esercitare la massima attenzione ed il massimo controllo Ogni reparto deve essere messo a punto, dalla tessitura, all'orditura, alla rifinizione. Inoltre stiamo potenziando il servizio e ampliando la ricerca.

La tipologia di prodotti è cambiata in questa nuova realtà?

No, e questa è la scelta più importante che abbiamo fatto quest'anno. La nostra attenzione è sempre puntata sul cashmere, ed in questo senso siamo stati premiati da richieste importanti da parte di grossi compratori come Armani, Aquascutum, Escada. Ma in genere curiamo molto le fibre pregiate, camel, alpaca, angora... senza dimenticare i tessuti in pura lana di cui abbiamo un campionario ricchissimo.

Che collezione presenta il Lanificio del Casentino per la primavera-estate?

A rischio di essere monotoni, abbiamo riconfermato le nostre specializzazioni arricchendole di qualità e di performance. Non a caso le nostre collezioni si chiamano "Lana" e "Lana e...". Cioè da una parte un campionario più sempre lana e dall'altra le mischie nobili abbiamo fatto dei lana-seta, lana-seta-mohair, lana-lino lana-lino-seta-viscosa, ma sempre lana o della migliore. In questo campo stiamo facendo una grossa ricerca e a Prato Expo presentiamo una lana "effetto vegetale" dove il classico sposa le ultime tecnologie, con un effetto molto interessante.

Come vanno gli affari all'estero?

A Colonia è andata molto bene, incominciamo a ricevere ora le prime telefonate, le prime proposte...anche se quest'anno i tedeschi hanno rischiato bene poco, a differenza degli altri anni. Non male l' America, che con il Giappone e la Cina fa ormai parte del nostro quotidiano. Stiamo approfondendo il discorso con i Paesi dell'Est... Li ci sono solo 4-5 grandi confederazioni che stanno piano piano mettendo a punto le loro collezioni per la Germania. Abbiamo preso contatti con Polonia e Cecoslovacchia, ma i risultati si vedranno a fine stagione. La Turchia invece sta andando molto bene: confezione per Germania e Bielorussia, richiede tessuti pregiati. Per quanto sia un anno difficile, questo, per tutta la produzione tessile, posso dirmi abbastanza soddisfatto.

It is 8 o'clock in the morning. The Lanificio awakes to the incessant noise of its machines and to the footsteps of Alfio Aldrovandi whom we meet while he is savouring his first hot black coffee. Now aged 47, with 30 years experience in the textile industry - nine of them with the Lanificio del Casentino - he now manages this business with the ability of an entrepreneur a maturity which derives from a long commitment to this field.

At what point are we with production, Mr. Aldrovandi?

The Lanificio del Casentino now concentrates on the medium, medium-high range, with 2,5 million sale covered the slightest error. Our greatest effort at the present time is, therefore, to improve, in every sense. All those who work here must be very aware of this new reality, they must pay the greatest attention and exert the maximum control. Every department must be 'on alert' from the texturing to the warping, and on to the finishing touches. Besides this, we are strengthening our service and widening our research.

Has the type of product changed in this new reality?

No. And this is the most important choice that we have made this year. Our attention is always on cashmere and in this regard we have been rewarded by very important requests on the part of large buyers like Armani, Aquascutum, Escada. We generally deal in high quality fibres, camel, alpaca, angora, without forgetting our vast selection of fabrics in pure wool.

What is the Lanificio del Casentino presenting for their Spring-Summer Collection?

At the risk of being monotonous, we have reaffirmed our specializations, enriching their quality and performance. It is not by chance that we have entitled our Collections 'Wool' and 'Wool and...'. This means that some of our samples are 100% wool and others a rich mixture. We have produced wool-silk; wool-silk-mohair; wool-linen; wool-viscose; but always wool and of the best quality. We are conducting wide research in this sector and at Prato Expo we are presenting a 'vegetable effect' wool where the classic blends with the latest technology offering very interesting results.

How is business abroad?

In Cologne everything went very well. We are just beginning to receive our first telephone calls - the first proposals. Even if the German clients have risked very little this year compared to others. We can classified America as 'not bad' as they together with Japan and China, make up part of our daily contacts. We are deepening our relationships with Eastern European countries. There are only about 4 or 5 large garment makers there who are, little by little, putting together collections for Germany. We have frequent contact with Poland and Czecoslovakia but any results here will be seen at the end of the season. Turkey is going well: they make garments for Germany and Bielorussia, richer materials are in demand here. Even though it is a difficult year for all textile production, I consider myself satisfied.

INTERVISTA/INTERVIEW
Judith Wilson

PRONTO
SIGNORA WILSON,
MI SENTE
SIGNORA WILSON?

011
HAND MADE GROUP
LANIFICIO DEL CASENTINO NEWS

News
LANIFICIO DEL CASENTINO

Our second issue One hundred and fifty
years Anniversary The market at the
millenium's end Trends for Spring Summer
'99 The new collection at Prato Expo
Vogue Tessuti on Lanificio del Casentino
Oliviero Toscani on Utopia and other
projects Interviews. And more...

©150

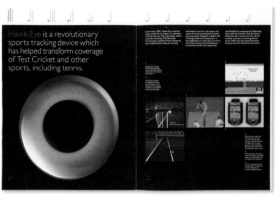

Hawk-Eye is a revolutionary sports tracking device which has helped transform coverage of Test Cricket and other sports, including tennis.

Venner TV is one of the world's top producers of Cycling and Badminton events. VTV produces and distributes its programmes around the world.

012
ROSE DESIGN ASSOCIATES
TELEVISION CORPORATION
CORPORATE BROCHURE

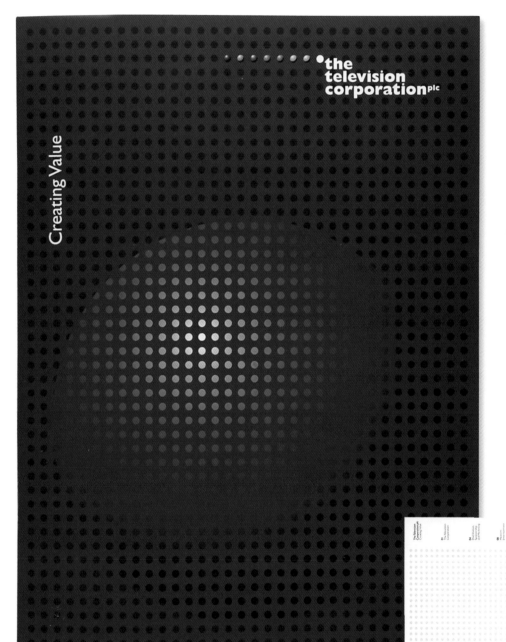

Creating Value

the television
corporation plc

The Television Corporation is the UK's leading independent supplier of programmes to broadcasters worldwide. Combining two of Britain's largest production companies, Mentorn and Sunset+Vine, with one of the UK's most respected production facilities operations, The Television Corporation is a fast-growing media business. The Group produces over 3000 hours of television each year for all the UK's major television channels, distributing them to around 200 countries . . . .

ART DIRECTOR:
SIMON ELLIOTT

DESIGNER:
SIMON ELLIOTT

PHOTOGRAPHERS:
PAUL ZAK
LOL KEEGAN

CLIENT:
TELEVISION
CORPORATION PLC

SOFTWARE:
ILLUSTRATOR
PHOTOSHOP
QUARKXPRESS

MATERIALS:
VALLIANT GLOSS
ART

PRINTING:
OFFSET LITHO

UK

FEEL THE RUSH

↘FOR TRUE LOVERS OF SPORT AND THE OUTDOOR WORLD. ↘ THIS CENTRE OF EXCELLENCE COVERING A BROAD RANGE OF SPORTS AND OUTDOOR PURSUITS WILL PROVIDE A REWARDING LEISURE EXPERIENCE IN A STIMULATING, ATMOSPHERIC AND VIBRANT ENVIRONMENT. ↘ INCORPORATES A NUMBER OF THEMED ATTRACTIONS AND 'TRY OUT' ZONES TO GIVE VISITORS A BROADER AND MORE ENJOYABLE VISIT ↘ TARGETED AT THE NEW UPWARDLY MOBILE GENERATION OF TIME PRECIOUS A, B, C1 CUSTOMERS DISILLUSIONED BY BLAND, CLINICAL AND STRESSFUL RETAIL VENUES. ↘ OFFERS AGGLOMERATION BENEFITS TO SMALLER SPECIALIST SPORTS AND OUTDOOR RETAILERS WHO CAN DEMONSTRATE PROVEN TECHNICAL EXPERTISE AND BACK UP. ↘ AN INTERACTIVE SPORTS CONCEPT FOR THE 21ST CENTURY, EMBRACING E.COMMERCE AND TECHNOLOGY, LAUNCHING AS A TRUE 'CLICKS AND MORTAR' LEISURE CONCEPT.

The 1990s witnessed a major change in lifestyles, a more fluid and mobile society placing a far greater emphasis on leisure pursuits, health and fitness. This increased mobility combined with higher disposable incomes and a time precious 25–40 age group, expressed itself with the emergence of adrenaline sports into the mainstream market.

In parallel with this increased commitment to sports and leisure activity the 1990s saw the growth of multiple sports stores in large in town and out of town locations often at the expense of smaller specialist independent retailers. The late 1990s also saw the emergence of specialist retail chains from the fragmented outdoor sporting goods market but often within small stores offering restricted ranges.

Sportsfactory offers smaller specialist independents and larger brand owners the opportunity to locate together within an innovative leisure complex. Operators will gain substantial economies of scale through increased marketing exposure and pedestrian traffic, without compromising levels of service and brand integrity.

ART DIRECTOR:
ATTIK

DESIGNER:
ATTIK

PHOTOGRAPHER:
ATTIK

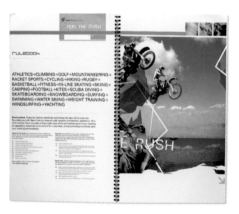

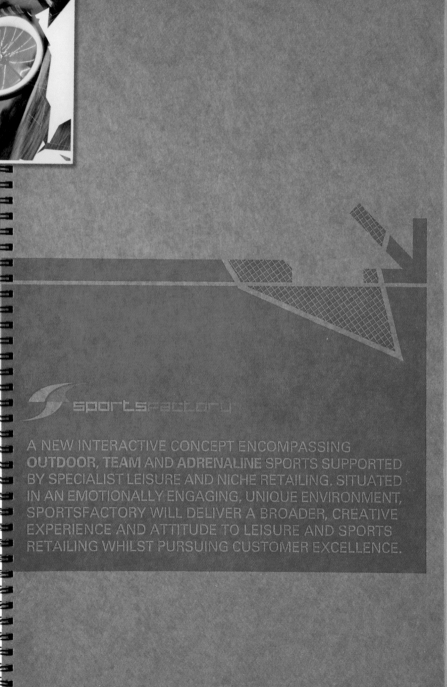

sportsfactory

A NEW INTERACTIVE CONCEPT ENCOMPASSING OUTDOOR, TEAM AND ADRENALINE SPORTS SUPPORTED BY SPECIALIST LEISURE AND NICHE RETAILING. SITUATED IN AN EMOTIONALLY ENGAGING, UNIQUE ENVIRONMENT, SPORTSFACTORY WILL DELIVER A BROADER, CREATIVE EXPERIENCE AND ATTITUDE TO LEISURE AND SPORTS RETAILING WHILST PURSUING CUSTOMER EXCELLENCE.

ART DIRECTORS:
JACK ANDERSON
LARRY ANDERSON

DESIGNERS:
LARRY ANDERSON
BELINDA BOWLING
HOLLY CRAVEN
JAMES TEE
MICHAEL BRUGMAN

PHOTOGRAPHER:
ABRAMS
LACAGNINA STUDIO

CLIENT:
NOVELL INC

SOFTWARE:
QUARKXPRESS

MATERIALS:
COUGAR OPAQUE

PRINTING:
MACDONALD
PRINTING,
VANCOUVER

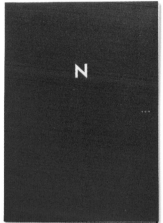

014

HORNALL ANDERSON
DESIGN WORKS
NOVELL 2002 CORPORATE BROCHURE

USA

"A retail site that lives up to its brick and mortar reputation."
—Access Magazine

SPOT ON

Nobody clicks past a Target TV spot. Our campaigns have been consistent hits on the small screen. Featuring product and Target style in unique and innovative ways. Fine-tuned creative, unexpectedly great soundtracks and topflight production all combine with merchandise that exceeds expectations. Just watch the results.

ART DIRECTOR:
CHERYL WATSON

DESIGNERS:
CHERYL WATSON
SHARON McKENDRY

CLIENT:
TARGET

| **015**
GRAPHICULTURE
TARGET BRAND BOOK & DVD

USA

TARGET.COM HITS THE DOT

Target is a bona fide power in e-commerce. Nielsen NetRatings consistently rank target.com among the top twenty retail sites for total monthly unique visitors.* And we consistently rank in the top five among unique visitors at home and at work, outpacing our competitors' shopping sites.

*Unique visitors are calculated monthly. One unique visitor is defined as one individual who visits a Web site during the month, regardless of the number of visits.

CHANGE. It's part and parcel of life. And at some point in all our lives, we have to face the overwhelming task of uprooting from the comfort and familiarity of our surroundings to start life anew elsewhere.

ART DIRECTOR: CHRISTOPHER LEE	DESIGNER: KAI	CLIENT: UTS FAMILY MOVERS	SOFTWARE: FREEHAND PHOTOSHOP	MATERIALS: MATT ARTPAPER	PRINTING: 4C X 4C

SINGAPORE

017
NB:STUDIO
MERCHANT HANDBOOK

ART DIRECTORS:
ALAN DYE
NICK FINNEY
BEN STOTT

DESIGNER:
NICK FINNEY

PHOTOGRAPHER:
NICK FINNEY

CLIENT:
MERCHANT

SOFTWARE AND
HARDWARE:
ILLUSTRATOR
PHOTOSHOP
QUARKXPRESS
SONY DIGITAL
CAMERA

MATERIALS:
IMAGINE 325/220GSM
NEW TAFFETA 280GSM
HELLO GLOSS 150GSM
KASKARD SPARROW
GREY 225GSM
XPOSE CLEAR 285GSM

PRINTING:
THE BEACON PRESS

UK

ART DIRECTOR:
FABIO ONGARATO

DESIGNERS:
STEFAN PIETSCH
YARRA LAURIE

CLIENT:
ELENBERG FRASER

MATERIALS:
PARILUX

PRINTING:
COLORCRAFT

AUSTRALIA

ELENBERG FRASER

ARCHITECTURE
374 GEORGE STREET FITZROY MELBOURNE VICTORIA 3065
AUSTRALIA
TEL +61 3 9417 2055 FAX +61 3 9417 2866
MAIN OFF – EF.COM.AU WWW.E-F.COM.AU

0205 Collins Hotel *Commercial development proposal, Melbourne Docklands 2002*
0204 Lion Headland *New house, Yaalong 2002–2004*
0203 Springvale Road *Office & distribution centre, Mulgrave 2002*
0202 Move-In *Commercial showroom, Melbourne 2002*
0201 Collins Gardens *Commercial development proposal, Melbourne Docklands 2002*
0102 Melbourne Foundation *Gallery structure, Melbourne 2001*
0101 Nixon House *House refurbishment & artists studio, Eltham 2001 2002*
0024 Kookaï *New store fit out, Richmond 2001*
0023 Kookaï *New store fit out, Chadstone 2001 2002*
0022 Watergate Place *Residential + commercial development, Melbourne Docklands 2001 2004*
0021 George & Argyle *New offices & showroom, Fitzroy 2001 2002*
0020 Kookaï *New store fit out Castle Towers, Sydney 2001*
0019 Kookaï *New store fit out (W.B, Sydney 2001*
0018 1324 *Commercial development, speculative proposal, Melbourne 2001*
0017 Sydney Town Hall *Competition entry, Sydney 2000*
0016 Theosophical Apartment *Penthouse apartment, Melbourne 2000*
0015 Webb Dock Bridge *Invited competition (short listed entry), Melbourne Docklands 2000*
0014 Hanover Foundation *Invited ideas competition, Melbourne 2000*
0013 Schwartz Beach House *House Refurbishment & Landscaping, Yaalong 2000*
0012 St Andrews Beach House *St Andrews Beach, Rye 2000*
0011 North East Stadium Precinct *Competition (winning entry), Melbourne Docklands 2000*
0010 Batman's Hill Precinct *Various sites, current shortlist, Melbourne Docklands 2000*
0009 Cheltenham *Warehouse refurbishment, Cheltenham 2000*
0008 Portsea Beach Apartments *Apartment planning proposal, Portsea 2000*
0005 Collins Street Lofts *Competition (short listed entry), Melbourne 2000*
9915 Queen Victoria Site *Competition (short listed entry), Melbourne 1999*
9911 TKTS2k *Ticket booth design competition, New York 1999*
9910 Hawthorn Tram Depot *Competition (short listed entry), Hawthorn 1999*
9909 Munro House *Extension and renovation, Hawthorn 1999 2002*
9908 International Dynamics *Office & warehousing, Richmond 1999 2000*
9907 Café-Hotel *Apartment conversion, North Melbourne 1999*
9906 Liberty Display Suite *Interiors prototype, Melbourne 1999*
9905 Apartment 1202 *Apartment fitout proposal, Melbourne 1999*
9904 Icon III *Office conversion, Richmond 1999*
9903 Icon II *Warehouse apartments, Richmond 1999*
9902 Museum of Modern Art at Heide *Competition entry, Melbourne 1998*
9901 Crumpet Factory *Warehouse apartments, Richmond 1999*
9817 Westgarth Duplex *Housing prototype, Westgarth 1998*
9816 Doncaster Park & Ride *Masterplanning studies, Doncaster 1998*
9815 House of the Future *Competition entry, Melbourne 1998*
9812 White Collar Pub *Prototype bar & café, Melbourne 1998*
9811 Mockridge Fountain *Competition entry, Melbourne 1998*
9810 Mainland Offices *Office fitout, Melbourne 1998*
9809 JCM Offices *Prototype office components, Brunswick 1998*
9808 Satellite Dish *Prototype bar & café, Melbourne 1998*
9807 Interdyn *Interior retail planning studies, Richmond 1998*
9805 Roof Garden *Extension & garden works, St Kilda 1998*
9804 Ferrari Bar *Interior studies, Melbourne 1998*
9803 Liberty Tower *Apartment building, Collins Street Melbourne 1998–2002*
9802 Icon I *Warehouse apartments, Richmond 1998*
9801 Leonardi Brandhouse *Advertising agency fit out, Richmond 1998*
9710 Shanghai Housing *Competition entry (commendation), Shanghai 1997*
9709 Docklands Northbank Displan *Speculative proposal, Melbourne 1997*
9708 Spencer Square *Competition (winning entry), Melbourne 1997*
9707 Seagull Paddock *Masterplanning studies, Geelong 1997*
9706 Federation Square *Design competition, Melbourne 1997*
9705 Batman's Hill Precinct *Melbourne Docklands 1997*
9704 St Kilda Station *Competition (short listed entry), St Kilda 1997*
9703 Surfworld *Masterplanning studies, Torquay 1997*
9702 St Johns Anglican Church site *Competition (winning entry), Camberwell 1998*
9701 Encel House *Extension and renovation, Williamstown 1997–2000*
9602 RMIT Sports Facility *Speculative proposal, Melbourne 1996*
9601 Dazzle Shed *Garden shed, Carlton 1996*

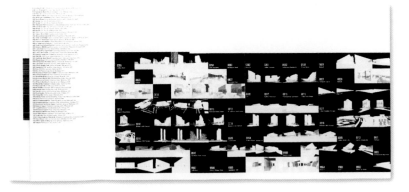

018
FABIO ONGARATO DESIGN
ELENBERG FRASER ARCHITECTS
COMPANY PROFILE

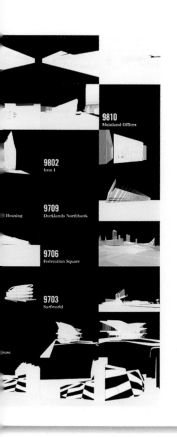

9810
Mainland Offices

9802
Icon I

9709
Docklands Northbank

9706
Federation Square

9703
Surfworld

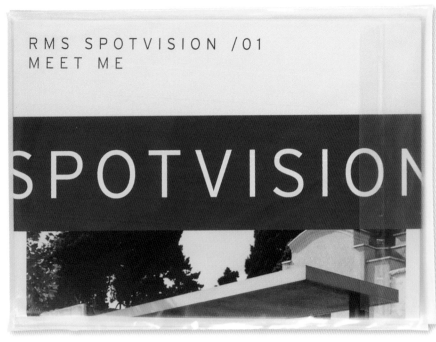

RMS SPOTVISION /01
MEET ME

SPOTVISION

ART DIRECTOR:
NIKOLAOS CHOTOS

DESIGNER:
NIKOLAOS CHOTOS

PHOTOGRAPHER:
NIKOLAOS CHOTOS

CLIENT:
RADIO MARKETING
SERVICE

SOFTWARE AND
HARDWARE:
QUARKXPRESS
MACINTOSH

MATERIALS:
BAVARIA

PRINTING:
4-COLOR +
SPOT COLOR

|019
CAMPAÑEROS
RMS SPOTVISION

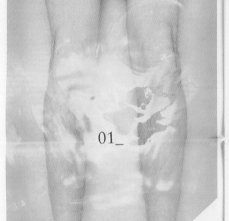

01_

01_ PPC – PRE PRODUCTION CALL

THESE_ *Eine intensive Vorbereitung in Abstimmung mit dem Produktionshaus spart Arbeit, Zeit und Geld.* ERKLÄRUNG_ *Mehr Professionalität wird durch eine gründliche Vorbereitung erreicht. Der PPC hilft allen am Funkspot Beteiligten dabei, Einzelheiten der Produktion im Vorfeld mit dem Tonmeister und dem Regisseur abzustimmen. Unter PPC ist also das PPM des Funks zu verstehen.* STATEMENT_ *„Ein Werbefilm wird gedreht. Location: Australien. Top-Regisseur, Top-Idee, Top-Budget. Vorbereitung über Wochen, wichtigster Termin: PPM; Meeting den ganzen Tag, jedes Detail wird geklärt, der Dreh kann beginnen. Ergebnis: ein Cannes-Löwe. Ein Funkspot wird produziert. Location: renommiertes Funk-studio vor Ort. Top-Tonmeister, Top-Idee, Budget vorhanden. Vorbereitung zwischen Tür und Angel, wichtigster Termin: recht-zeitig im Taxi zum Studio zu sitzen. Die Produktion kann begin-nen. Ergebnis: hätte besser sein können! Die Lösung: das PPM des Funks, der PPC. Alle Experten am Tisch, alle Details werden geklärt. Die Produktion kann beginnen. Ergebnis: Gold beim ADC. Denn: Gute Ideen müssen erstklassig umgesetzt werden. Das gilt auch für Funk!" Hubertus von Lobenstein*

05_

05_ INTERNATIONALE WETTBEWERBE

THESE_ *Auch in Deutschland gibt es gute Funkspots – sie brauchen nur mehr Auszeichnung.* ERKLÄRUNG_ *Mit guten Funkspots können Agenturen im Kreativ-Ranking richtig Gas geben. Und damit es nicht bei nationalem Ruhm bleibt, werden die Gewinner-Spots beim RAMSES ist gemacht, um an internationalen Wettbe-werben teilzunehmen. Hierfür spendiert die RMS eine englische Abmischung in einem Londoner Produktionshaus.* STATEMENT_ *„Seit unserem Symposium lohnt sich ein kreativer Funkspot für die Macher doppelt: Nicht nur auf inländischen Kreativ-Wettbewerben kann man in dieser Outsider-Disziplin leichter punkten (weil die Konkurrenz nicht so ausgeschlafen ist wie bei Print & TV), sondern zukünftig auch international. Denn die RMS sponsert den Gewinnern des RAMSES zukünftig einen Trip nach London in eins der besten Funkstudios zur Übersetzung der deutschen Produktion; für den Einsatz bei Wettbewerben rund um die Welt." Oliver Voss*

020
THIRTEEN DESIGN
BRISTOL LEGIBLE CITY:
FROM HERE TO THERE

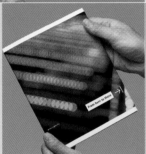

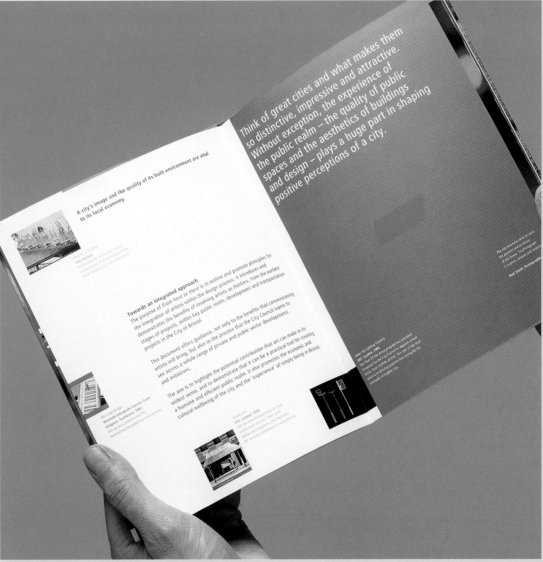

Think of great cities and what makes them so distinctive, impressive and attractive. Without exception, the experience of the public realm — the quality of public spaces and the aesthetics of buildings and design — plays a huge part in shaping positive perceptions of a city.

A city's image and the quality of its built environment are vital to its local economy.

Towards an integrated approach. The purpose of *From here to there* is to outline and promote principles for the integration of artists within the design process. It introduces and demonstrates the benefits of involving artists as thinkers, from the earliest stages of projects, within key public realm, development and transportation projects in the City of Bristol.

This document offers guidance, not only to the benefits that commissioning artists will bring, but also to the process that the City Council wants to see across a whole range of private and public sector developments and initiatives.

The aim is to highlight the potential contribution that art can make in its widest sense, and to demonstrate that it can be a practical tool for creating a humane and efficient public realm. It also promotes the economic and cultural wellbeing of the city and the 'experience' of simply being in Bristol.

ART DIRECTOR:	DESIGNERS:	PHOTOGRAPHER:	CLIENT:	SOFTWARE:	MATERIALS:	PRINTING:
HARRIET MILLER	HARRIET MILLER DANIELLE WAY	NICK SMITH	CITY ID	PHOTOSHOP QUARKXPRESS	ACCENT ECO WHITE PHOENIX MOTION	4-COLOR PROCESS + 1 SPECIAL + SPOT VARNISH + SEAL

↗ **Ways of Working**
Your work life, your life's work

|021
BOSTOCK & POLLITT
EMPLOYEE HANDBOOK

WOW

We profit
from our
principles

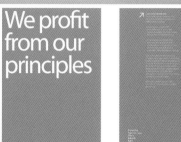

ART DIRECTOR:
JOHN ATKIN

DESIGNER:
JOHN ATKIN

CLIENT:
RABOBANK

SOFTWARE AND
HARDWARE:
QUARKXPRESS
MACINTOSH

FABIO ONGARATO DESIGN
TESKA & CARSON CORPORATE PROFILE

ART DIRECTOR: DESIGNER: CLIENT: MATERIALS: PRINTING:
FABIO ONGARATO   RYAN GUPPY   TESKA & CARSON   PARILUX   GUNN & TAYLOR

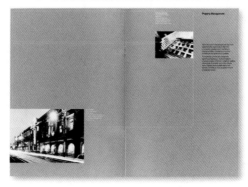

|023
ROSE DESIGN ASSOCIATES
WESTZONE LAUNCH BROCHURE

ART DIRECTOR:	DESIGNER:	PHOTOGRAPHER:	CLIENT:	SOFTWARE:	MATERIALS:	PRINTING:
SIMON ELLIOTT	SIMON ELLIOTT	PAUL ZAK	WESTZONE PUBLISHING LTD	ILLUSTRATOR PHOTOSHOP QUARKXPRESS	CYCLUS OFFSET VALLIANT GLOSS ART	OFFSET LITHO

UK

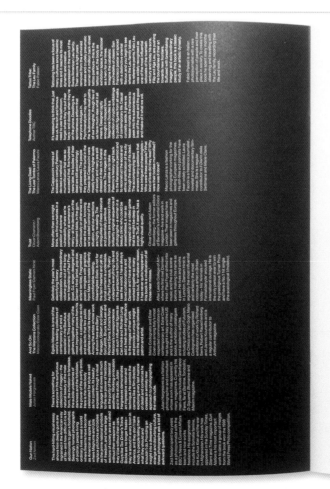

024
LAVA GRAPHIC DESIGNERS
LOST BOYS BROCHURE

ART DIRECTORS:	DESIGNERS:	PHOTOGRAPHER:	CLIENT:	SOFTWARE AND HARDWARE:	MATERIALS:	PRINTING:
HANS WOLBERS	HANS WOLBERS	VARIOUS	LOST BOYS	PHOTOSHOP	POP SET	KOENDERS &
LUIS MENDO	LUIS MENDO			QUARKXPRESS		VAN STIJN
ARJEN	ARJEN			MAC G4		
KLINKENBERG	KLINKENBERG					

ANNUAL REPORTS

LAVA GRAPHIC DESIGNERS // FABIO ONGARATO DESIGN // RADLEY YELDAR // SQUIRES & COMPANY // SALTERBAXTER // HAT-TRICK DESIGN // CAHAN & ASSOCIATES // FAUXPAS // EVOLVE // MUTABOR DESIGN // EMERY VINCENT DESIGN // 2D3D // VINJE DESIGN // SAS // METAL // ALLEMANN ALMQUIST & JONES // HORNALL ANDERSON DESIGN WORKS // KINETIC SINGAPORE // FROST DESIGN // CAMPAÑEROS // FOSTER DESIGN GROUP // CHIMERA DESIGN

.02

BBA GROUP

GROUP OVERVIEW 2001

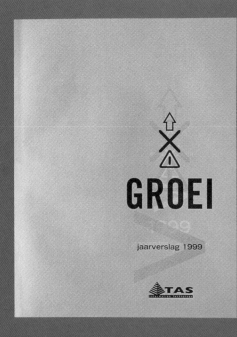

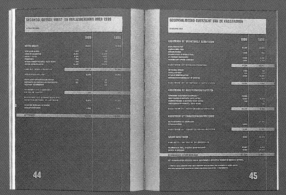

THE NETHERLANDS

DESIGNERS:
RITCHARD KELLIHER
HANS WOLBERS

CLIENT:
BJS BUSINESS
MEDIA BV

026

FABIO ONGARATO DESIGN
ARNOLD BLOCK LEIBLER
2002 YEAR IN REVIEW

AUSTRALIA

DESIGNER:
RYAN GUPPY

CLIENT:
ARNOLD BLOCK
LEIBLER

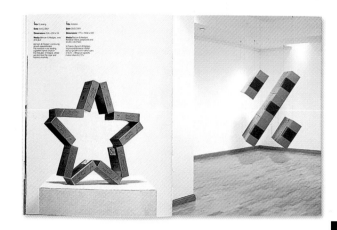

ART DIRECTOR:
ANDREW GORMAN

DESIGNER:
ROB RICHE

PHOTOGRAPHERS:
PAUL DIXON
ROB RICHE
JOHN EDWARDS

CLIENT:
GALLAHER GROUP
PLC

SOFTWARE AND
HARDWARE:
PHOTOSHOP
QUARKXPRESS
MAC

MATERIALS:
MANNO ART MATT

PRINTING:
6-COLOR LITHO
CTD CAPITA

027
RADLEY YELDAR
GALLAHER ANNUAL
REPORT 2000

Gallaher Group Plc
Annual Review and Summary
Financial Statement 2000

USA

DESIGNER:	PHOTOGRAPHER:	CLIENT:	SOFTWARE AND	MATERIALS:	PRINTING:
BRANDON MURPHY	VARIOUS	BELLWETHER	HARDWARE:	DULCET/FRENCH	WILLIAMSON
		EXPLORATION	QUARKXPRESS		PRINTING
			MAC G4		

029
SALTERBAXTER
SOUND PRACTICE

Eco-efficiency
Using fewer resources, and wasting less of those we do use, makes economic as well as environmental sense.

COMPARED TO 1995, WE NOW USE 33 PERCENT FEWER SOLVENTS AND GENERATE 45 PERCENT LESS HAZARDOUS WASTE AND 32 PERCENT LESS POLYCARBONATE SCRAP FOR EVERY UNIT OF PRODUCT THAT WE MANUFACTURE.

Solvent use
(litres 000s)

Solvent use
(litres/million units of output)
■ 2001 Actual
□ Targets 01 & 02

Hazardous waste
(tonnes)

Hazardous waste
(tonnes/million units of output)
■ 2001 Actual
□ Targets 01 & 02

Polycarbonate scrap
(tonnes)

Polycarbonate scrap
(tonnes/million units of CD output)
■ 2001 Actual
□ Targets 01 & 02

Ozone depletion
Purchases of CFCs & HCFCs
(kilogrammes)
■ HCFCs
□ CFCs

SOUND PRACTICE

Our impact
All aspects of our business use resources and create waste. Manufacturing is an area where we have undertaken formal reviews of the impacts resulting from this, and closely monitored our performance against some key indicators.

Our manufacturing sites use raw materials including polycarbonate, aluminium, solvents and inks. We continually strive to improve the efficiency of the process and minimise the quantity of material which is wasted, at the same time reducing the environmental impact caused by the wastes.

Some waste is inevitable. A proportion of the solvents used are emitted as vapours; these can present a health hazard in the working environment and contribute to smog formation when released to the atmosphere. Water-based effluents are treated on site and then discharged to sewer for further treatment. Any waste that can't be recycled, including hazardous waste, is sent for external disposal at landfill sites or incinerators.

We also use ozone depleting substances across our businesses, in air-conditioning and some fire protection systems. If released, these substances will damage the ozone layer.

Our performance
Solvents
We made good progress in solvent reduction, achieving a 31% drop in the quantity used and a 24% reduction per million units output (pmuo). This was significantly better than our target reduction of 5% pmuo.

The improvements were mainly due to a change of solvent specification at Uden (Netherlands) and improved controls at Jacksonville (US).

Hazardous waste
We reduced hazardous waste by 7%. This was equivalent to a 3% increase pmuo and fell short of our target 10% reduction pmuo. The main reason for this was the deferral of a new waste water treatment plant at Uden (now installed).

Polycarbonate efficiency
Procedural improvements at Toshiba-EMI (Japan) and Jacksonville contributed to a 16% reduction in polycarbonate scrap, equivalent to 10% pmuo. This was better than our 5% reduction target.

Ozone depleters
We record purchases of ozone depleting substances. No CFCs or halons were purchased. Purchases of HCFCs, used to maintain existing units or install new ones, increased by 5%. We also purchased 170kgs of HFCs as replacements for HCFCs. These gases are ozone friendly but have a high global warming potential.

4

5

UK

ART DIRECTOR:
PENNY BAXTER

DESIGNER:
IVAN ANGELL

ILLUSTRATOR:
IVAN ANGELL

CLIENT:
THE EMI GROUP

SOFTWARE AND
HARDWARE:
QUARKXPRESS
MAC

MATERIALS:
CYCLUS OFFSET

PRINTING:
LITHO +
LETTERPRESS

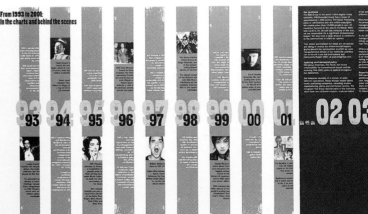

|030
SALTERBAXTER
TODAY... TOMORROW

ART DIRECTOR:
ALAN DELGADO

DESIGNER:
IVAN ANGELL

ILLUSTRATOR:
MARION DEUCHARS

CLIENT:
ACAMBIS PLC

SOFTWARE AND
HARDWARE:
QUARKXPRESS
MAC

MATERIALS:
NATURALIS ARCTIC
WHITE

PRINTING:
LITHO

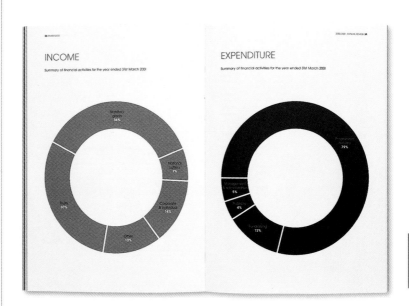

INCOME

Summary of financial activities for the year ended 31st March 2001

EXPENDITURE

Summary of financial activities for the year ended 31st March 2001

UK

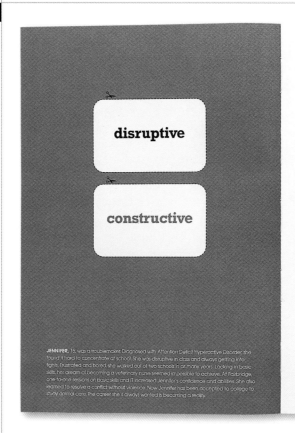

disruptive

constructive

JENNIFER, 15, was a troublemaker. Diagnosed with Attention Deficit Hyperactive Disorder, she found it hard to concentrate at school. She was disruptive in class and always getting into fights. Frustrated and bored, she walked out of two schools in as many years. Lacking in basic skills, her dream of becoming a veterinary nurse seemed impossible to achieve. At Fairbridge, one-to-one sessions on basic skills and IT increased Jennifer's confidence and abilities. She also learned to resolve a conflict without violence. Now Jennifer has been accepted to college to study animal care, the career she's always wanted is becoming a reality.

DESIGNER:
HAT-TRICK DESIGN

CLIENT:
FAIRBRIDGE

SOFTWARE:
QUARKXPRESS

MATERIALS:
ODYSSEY

PRINTING:
LITHO

ART DIRECTOR:
BILL CAHAN

DESIGNER:
KEVIN ROBERSON

ILLUSTRATOR:
KEVIN ROBERSON

CLIENT:
GATX CAPITAL
CORPORATION

MATERIALS:
STARWHITE
VICKSLAVERSTIARA

PRINTING:
H. MACDONALD

TB2B

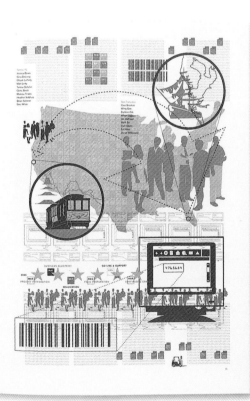

032
CAHAN & ASSOCIATES
GATX 2000 ANNUAL REPORT

ART DIRECTOR:
MARTIN STILLHART

DESIGNER:
MARTIN STILLHART

ILLUSTRATOR:
MARTIN STILLHART

CLIENT:
VEREIN JOB

SOFTWARE AND
HARDWARE:
QUARKXPRESS
MAC

MATERIALS:
Z-OFFSET W

PRINTING:
OFFSET

JAHRESBERICHT 2001 VEREIN JOB

Anforderungen der Ausbildungsbetriebe
Wünsche der Auszubildenden

033
FAUXPAS
VEREIN JOB ANNUAL REPORT

Seite 9

Finance 1999/2000
How your money was spent

Auditors' statement

The Harrow Partnership was established in 1998, bringing together the council and private, public and community and voluntary organisations to provide better services and improve the quality of life for local residents through a programme of exploiting every possible opportunity for joint working.

Making a difference together
Mary Whitty, Chief Executive, is a member of the Partnership Steering Group, comprising key local agencies, which steers the overall development of the Partnership.

The Partnership consists of four themes: health and social care, environment and economy, lifelong learning, and strengthening communities. Each theme has a strategy group to agree and monitor the priorities for joint working; and also periodically holds stakeholder forums to consult and receive proposals from a larger group of stakeholders.

The partnership also stages an annual conference as well as community events.

The Health and Social Care Strategy Group includes representation from the Health Authority, as well as the principal NHS Trusts, the local authority, Primary Care Groups, the CHC, voluntary groups, Carers and representatives from cultural communities. The Partnership is, therefore, an inclusive one, bringing together the interests of both service users and providers.

A series of seven Strategy Development Groups (SDGs) plan and develop health and social care services for different client groups. The groups devise strategic plans to meet identified needs, agree action plans and monitor progress.

Membership is from across both statutory and non statutory agencies. Strategy Development Groups have a key responsibility to develop the effective involvement of users, Carers, voluntary organisations and cultural communities in their work programmes, drawing on their experience and expertise to enrich the quality of joint planning in Harrow.

Prior to issuing the plan this year, a leaflet was sent to every Harrow resident asking them to identify their most important issues. Improving health emerged overall as second only to reducing crime of the 36 issues identified, with children's health, older people's health, diabetes, coronary heart disease, strokes and cancer seen as particularly important.

One of the virtues of the Partnership is that partners can be involved across a wider spectrum of activities. The Health Authority is also represented on each of the other three Partnership Groups and is, therefore, playing an active part in joint working on areas such as tackling poverty, enhancing the environment and harnessing the benefits of information and communication technology.

1 **Service users and patients**
To provide good quality health and social care services, ensuring that promoting independence and community involvement are integral to service planning and delivery.

2 **Supporting Carers**
To provide practical support to Carers and to involve Carers and their representative organisations in service planning.

3 **The community**
To start to address inequalities in health and the underlying causes of poor health (including poor housing and low income), to meet the healthcare needs of all sections of the community and to develop further the capacity of local voluntary organisations to provide services.

4 **Children and young people**
To improve the life chances of children and young people.

The four areas chosen as priority actions for the health and social care theme of the Harrow Partnership in 2000/2001

14   15

034
EVOLVE
NHS: BRENT AND HARROW
ANNUAL REPORT

UK

ART DIRECTOR:
DONNA HOUGHTON

DESIGNER:
JONATHAN HAWKES

CLIENT:
NHS: BRENT +
HARROW

SOFTWARE AND
HARDWARE:
QUARKXPRESS
MAC G4

PRINTING:
2-COLOR LITHO

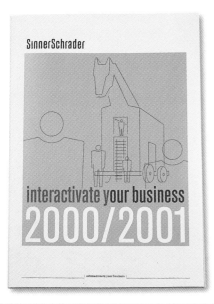

ART DIRECTOR:
JOHANNES PLASS

DESIGNER:
CHRISTIAN DWORAK

ILLUSTRATOR/
PHOTOGRAPHER:
CARSTEN RAFFEL

CLIENT:
SINNER SCHRADER

MATERIALS:
ZANDERS MEDLEY
PURE

PRINTING:
DRUCKEREI
HARTUNG

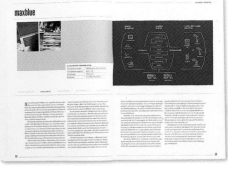

035
MUTABOR DESIGN
SINNER SCHRADER ANNUAL REPORT

ART DIRECTOR:
EMERY VINCENT
DESIGN

DESIGNER:
EMERY VINCENT
DESIGN

CLIENT:
LEIGHTON
HOLDINGS

AUSTRALIA

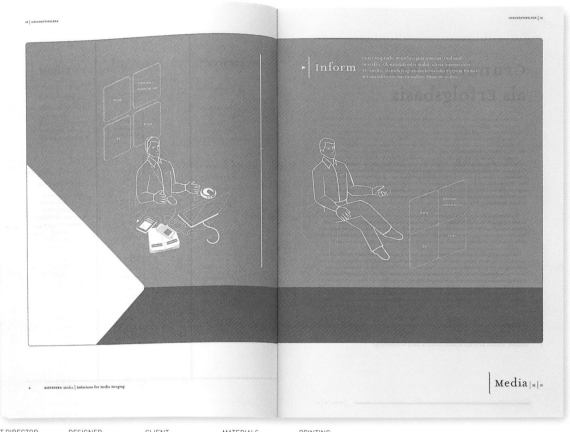

ART DIRECTOR:
JOHANNES PLASS

DESIGNER:
SIMONE CAMPE

CLIENT:
DISTEFORA
HOLDING

MATERIALS:
ZANDERS MEDLEY
PURE

PRINTING:
DRUCKEREI
HARTUNG

GERMANY

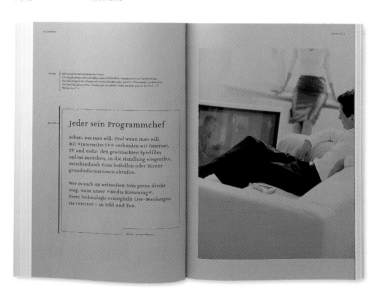

SVB

Persoonlijke
ontwikkeling
Plezier
Samenwerken

THE NETHERLANDS

ART DIRECTORS:	DESIGNERS:	PHOTOGRAPHER:	CLIENT:	SOFTWARE AND	MATERIALS:	PRINTING:
TIEMEN HARDER	TIEMEN HARDER	STAFF OF SOCIALE	SOCIALE	HARDWARE:	INVERCOTE ALBATO	OFFSET, 4-PROCESS
YEW-KEE CHUNG	YEW-KEE CHUNG	VERZEKERINGSBANK	VERZEKERINGSBANK	PHOTOSHOP	250GSM + OXFORD	COLORS
				QUARKXPRESS	120GSM	
				MAC		

Sociaal Jaarverslag 2001 > Sociale Verzekeringsbank (SVB)

537 Reacties

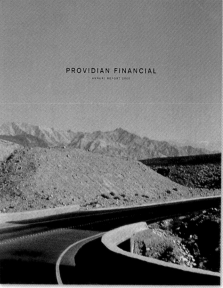

ART DIRECTOR:
BILL CAHAN

DESIGNER:
BOB DINETZ

CLIENT:
PROVIDIAN
FINANCIAL

SOFTWARE:
ILLUSTRATOR
PHOTOSHOP
QUARKXPRESS

MATERIALS:
UTOPIA 2 DULL

PRINTING:
LITHOGRAPHIX

04

PLEA-
SAN-
TON,
CA

USA

039
CAHAN & ASSOCIATES
PROVIDIAN 2000 ANNUAL REPORT

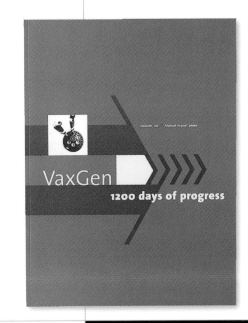

VaxGen, Inc | Annual Report 2000

VaxGen
1200 days of progress

ART DIRECTOR:
ANDREAS KELLER

DESIGNER:
ANDREAS KELLER

PHOTOGRAPHER:
JAMES CHIANG

CLIENT:
VAXGEN, INC

SOFTWARE AND
HARDWARE:
QUARKXPRESS
MAC

MATERIALS:
FRENCH PAPER
SMART WHITE

PRINTING:
ANDERSON
LITHOGRAPH

USA

"After years of working on preclinical studies with animal models, I came to VaxGen because the company is applying all the years of animal research to human testing. That is the only way to determine if a vaccine is effective in preventing infection in people, and the only way we will ever develop a vaccine."

Riri Shibata, D.V.M., Ph.D.
Scientist

"Helping to take VaxGen public in 1999 was a once-in-a-lifetime opportunity. But I am equally gratified by the work we have accomplished in developing the infrastructure for a public company and ensuring that our development projects continue on time and on budget."

Carter Lee, M.B.A.
Senior Vice President
Finance & Administration

"As founder of the International Vaccine Institute, I have seen how important proactive international development campaigns are for vaccines. That's why we're putting so much effort here on working with international agencies such as UNAIDS, the World Health Organization and the World Bank, as well as and private foundations, to plan for the introduction and distribution of AIDSVAX if it proves effective."

Seung-il Shin, Ph.D.
Senior Advisor
International Development

"The success so far of our trials has established us as a leader in AIDS vaccine clinical development. As the first company to conduct Phase III trials for an AIDS vaccine, we realized we had a special responsibility, especially to the volunteers. That's why we designed safety protocols and ethical practices that we believe set a new standard for clinical trials. I think it's a big reason why the trials have progressed so well."

Karin Orelind
Clinical Program Manager

"VaxGen has proved the skeptics wrong at every step. They said you couldn't protect chimps against HIV. We did. They said we'd fall in Phase I and II trials. We didn't. Then they said we'd never be able to enroll the Phase III trials and even if we did we'd have trouble keeping volunteers. Wrong again. But I guess they don't call it conventional wisdom for nothing."

William Heyward, M.D., M.P.H.
Vice President
International Clinical Research

12

13

040
VINJE DESIGN INC
VAXGEN ANNUAL REPORT 2000

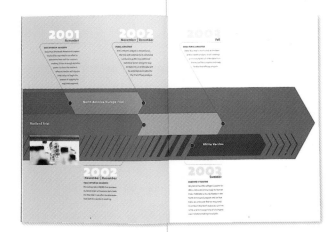

DIFFICULT TIMES. FOR US.
FOR EVERYONE ELSE.
So what did we do?

WE STRENGTHENED OUR
POSITION. WE BOUGHT WELL:
STRATEGIC ACQUISITIONS.
WE CUT COSTS. WE GREW
SALES. WE DID BETTER
THAN OUR COMPETITORS.

And what will we do next?

WE'LL CONTINUE: TO
GROW OUR SERVICES,
OUR BUSINESSES AND
THE MARKETS THAT WE'RE
IN. WE'LL CONTINUE TO
CREATE VALUE. MAKING
MORE OF WHAT WE HAVE.

041
SAS
BBA GROUP
ANNUAL REPORT 2001

UK

BBA GROUP
GROUP OVERVIEW 2001

ART DIRECTOR:	DESIGNER:	CLIENT:	SOFTWARE:	MATERIALS:	PRINTING:
DAVID STOCKS	MARTIN BROWN	BBA GROUP	QUARKXPRESS	MEGA MATT	WESTERHAM PRESS

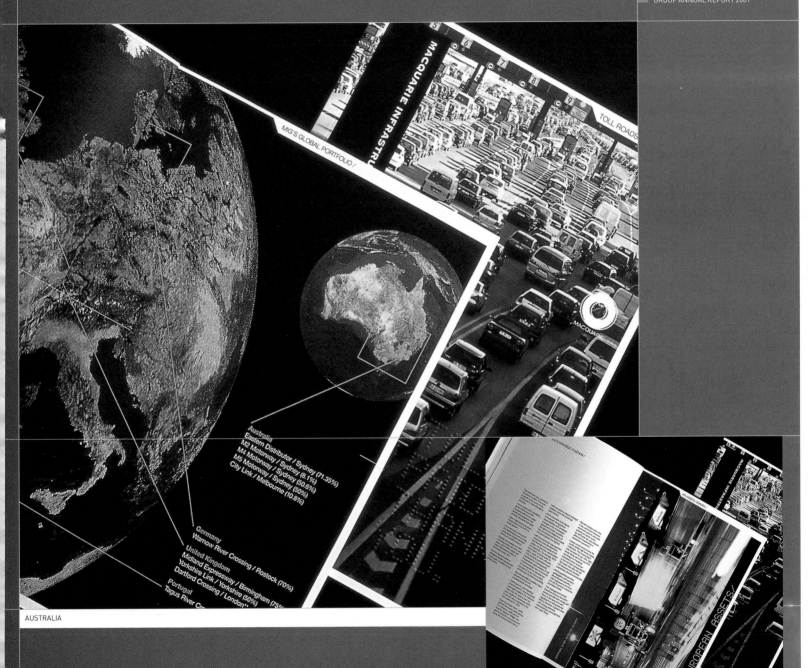

MIG'S GLOBAL PORTFOLIO /

MACQUARIE INFRASTRUCTURE

TOLL ROADS

Australia
Eastern Distributor / Sydney (71.35%)
M2 Motorway / Sydney (8.1%)
M4 Motorway / Sydney (50.6%)
M5 Motorway / Sydney (50%)
City Link / Melbourne (10.8%)

Germany
Warnow River Crossing / Rostock (70%)

United Kingdom
Midland Expressway / Birmingham
Yorkshire Link / Yorkshire (50%)
Dartford Crossing / London**

Portugal
Tagus River Cro

AUSTRALIA

ART DIRECTOR:
EMERY VINCENT
DESIGN

DESIGNER:
EMERY VINCENT
DESIGN

CLIENT:
MACQUARIE
INFRASTRUCTURE
GROUP

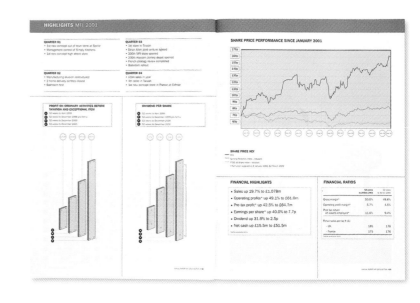

ART DIRECTORS:
MIKE HALL
GILMAR WENDT

DESIGNER:
EMMA SLATER

ILLUSTRATORS:
ROGER TAYLOR
JOHN SEE

CLIENT:
MFI GROUP

SOFTWARE:
QUARKXPRESS

MATERIALS:
COLORITE

PRINTING:
FULMAR

UK

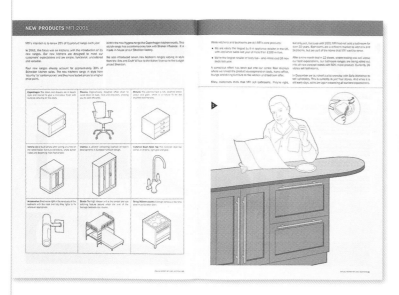

043

SAS
MFI GROUP 2001
ANNUAL REPORT

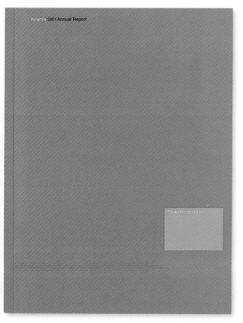

Valentis 2001 Annual Report

Statistics don't Lie

USA

Melanoma:
1 in 97

Restenosis
1 in 5

ART DIRECTOR:
BILL CAHAN

DESIGNER:
SHARRIE BROOKS

CLIENT:
VALENTIS

MATERIALS:
UTOPIA 2 DULL 80#

PRINTING:
COLOR GRAPHICS

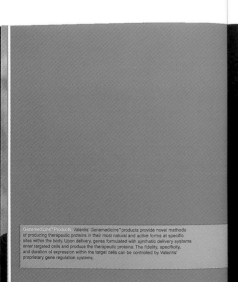

Genemedicine™ Products Valentis' Genemedicine™ products provide novel methods of producing therapeutic proteins in their most natural and active forms at specific sites within the body. Upon delivery, genes formulated with synthetic delivery systems enter targeted cells and produce the therapeutic proteins. The fidelity, specificity, and duration of expression within the target cells can be controlled by Valentis' proprietary gene regulation systems.

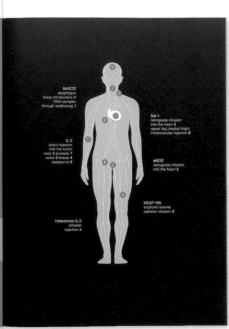

MnSOD
esophagus
bolus introduction of
DNA complex
through swallowing 1

Del-1
retrograde infusion
into the heart 3
upper leg (medial thigh)
intramuscular injection 8

IL-2
direct injection
into the tumor
neck 2 prostate 7
colon 6 breast 4
melanoma 9

eNOS
retrograde infusion
into the heart 3

VEGF-165
localized arterial
catheter infusion 3

Intravenous IL-2
infusion
injection 5

044
CAHAN & ASSOCIATES
VALENTIS 2001 ANNUAL REPORT

IN THE BEGINNING

30 YEARS LATER

STRATEGIC VISION

FINANCIAL FOCUS

045
METAL
20/20 ANNUAL REPORT

20/20

CAMDEN 2001 ANNUAL REPORT

20/20

ART DIRECTOR:	DESIGNERS:	CLIENT:	SOFTWARE AND	MATERIALS:	PRINTING:
PEAT JARIYA	PEAT JARIYA	CAMDEN	HARDWARE:	PLASTIC	AW
	GABE SCHREIBER		ILLUSTRATOR	CAMELOT	
			PAGEMAKER	LYNX	
			PHOTOSHOP		
			MAC G4		

Real PLACES

USA

Real VALUE

As long as there are shoppers and family dinners, as long as there is a need for real places, we will be building them and creating experiences that add value to customers' lives and build value for our shareholders. This value creation is apparent in our strong operating performance, growing development portfolio and recently increased dividend. There is no fluff, no fantasy, no fuzzy math. Just honest-to-goodness profits, reliable dividends and a rock solid company.

ART DIRECTOR:
JAN ALMQUIST

DESIGNERS:
JAN ALMQUIST
LINNAE DESILVA

PHOTOGRAPHER:
VARIOUS

CLIENT:
PENNSYLVANIA
REAL ESTATE
INVESTMENT TRUST

SOFTWARE AND
HARDWARE:
ILLUSTRATOR
PHOTOSHOP
QUARKXPRESS
MAC G4

MATERIALS:
MOHAWK
SUPERFINE
TEXT/COVER

Real LIFE

Hard Disk Drives

2001 Worldwide Desktop Disk Drive Market Share

Maxtor 34.3%

Maxtor led the industry in shipments of hard disk drives in 2001. During the year, we shipped a total of 45.1 million hard drives. The majority of these drives were for use in desktop computer systems.

Success in the desktop disk drive market is driven by quality products, customer service, and leading time-to-market and time-to-volume production. These have long been Maxtor's core strengths. In 2001, Maxtor was again the leader in time-to-volume shipments of the 40 gigabyte

per platter drive, introducing and shipping the product in June. The 40 gigabyte per platter drive was the industry "sweet spot" in the second half of 2001 and over 90% of our desktop drive shipments were at this configuration in the fourth quarter.

We offer a broad line of hard disk drives for the desktop. From our cost optimized single head/single platter drive to our industry leading four platter 160 gigabyte capacity product, Maxtor drives are designed to meet a range of needs on desktop computers. We also continue to

THE FUTURE

2002 and Beyond

Maxtor 2001

USA

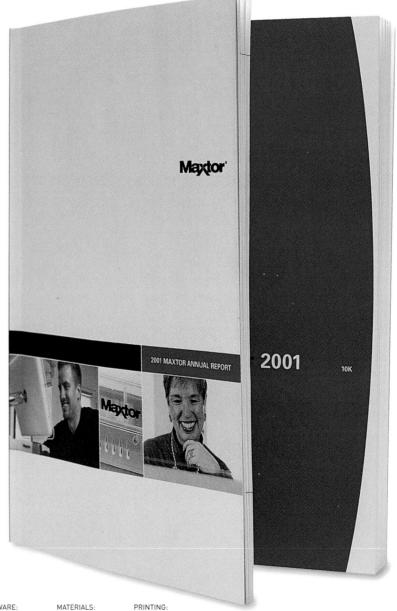

047
HORNALL ANDERSON
DESIGN WORKS
MAXTOR 2001 ANNUAL REPORT

ART DIRECTOR:
LISA CERVENY

DESIGNERS:
LISA CERVENY
ANDREW WICKLUND

PHOTOGRAPHER:
ALAN ABRAMOWITZ

CLIENT:
MAXTOR

SOFTWARE:
ILLUSTRATOR
PHOTOSHOP
QUARKXPRESS

MATERIALS:
80# COUGAR
OPAQUE +
60# COUGAR
OPAQUE

PRINTING:
WOODS
LITHOGRAPHICS

048

CAHAN & ASSOCIATES
BRE PROPERTIES 2001
ANNUAL REPORT

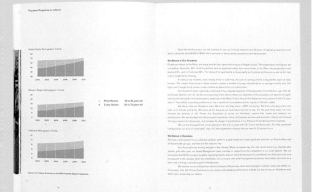

ART DIRECTOR:
BILL CAHAN

DESIGNER:
KEVIN ROBERSON

CLIENT:
BRE PROPERTIES

SOFTWARE:
PHOTOSHOP
QUARKXPRESS

MATERIALS:
COUGAR VELLUM

PRINTING:
HEMLOCK
PRINTERS

USA

THEIR PERFECT DREAM HOUSE ISN'T A HOUSE AT ALL.

amara holdings limited annual report 2001 **Ascend**

Ascend

SINGAPORE

ART DIRECTORS:
LENG SOH
PANN LIM
ROY POH

DESIGNERS:
LENG SOH
PANN LIM
ROY POH

ILLUSTRATORS:
LENG SOH
PANN LIM
ROY POH

CLIENT:
AMARA SINGAPORE

SOFTWARE AND
HARDWARE:
FREEHAND
PHOTOSHOP
MAC

MATERIALS:
ART PAPER + MAN-
MADE GRASS PATCH

PRINTING:
5CX5C + GLOSS
VARNISH

049
KINETIC SINGAPORE
ASCEND

Ascend

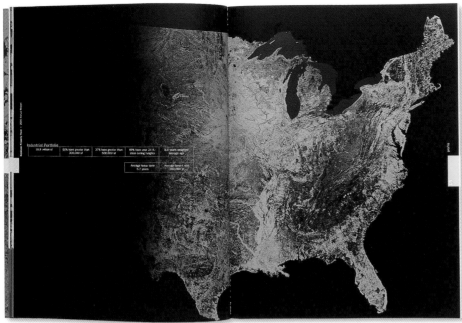

050
ALLEMANN ALMQUIST & JONES
KEYSTONE PROPERTY TRUST
ANNUAL REPORT 2000

ART DIRECTOR:
JAN ALMQUIST

DESIGNER:
ANNE WREN

PHOTOGRAPHER:
CAMERON
DAVIDSON

CLIENT:
KEYSTONE
PROPERTY TRUST

SOFTWARE AND
HARDWARE:
ILLUSTRATOR
PHOTOSHOP
QUARKXPRESS
MAC G4

MATERIALS:
POTLATCH MᶜCOY
GLOSS

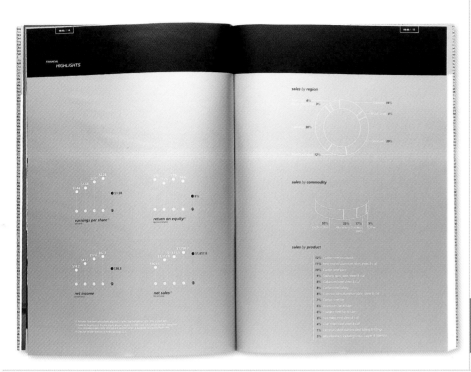

051

METAL
RS01

USA

ART DIRECTOR:
PEAT JARIYA

DESIGNERS:
PEAT JARIYA
GABE SCHREIBER

CLIENT:
RELIANCE STEEL
& ALU

SOFTWARE AND
HARDWARE:
ILLUSTRATOR
PAGEMAKER
PHOTOSHOP
MAC G4

MATERIALS:
POTLATCH MᶜCOY

PRINTING:
AW

onevision
of where we are going and how we will get there

2002 begins the 42nd year of consecutive quarterly
cash dividend payments to our shareholders.
Since our initial public offering in 1994, our dividend
payments have increased, in total, 440% and our
average annual return on shareholders' investment is
21% as of December 31, 2001.

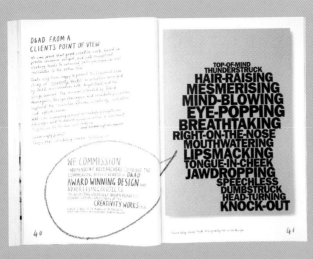

ART DIRECTOR:	DESIGNERS:	ILLUSTRATOR:	COPYWRITER:	CLIENT:	PAPER/MATERIALS:	PRINTING:
VINCE FROST	VINCE FROST	MARION DEUCHARS	HOWARD FLETCHER	D&AD BRITISH	PREMIER PAPER	VENTURA
	MARION DEUCHARS			DESIGN & ART	CLASSIC PAPER	
				DIRECTION	CYCLUS OFFSET	

UK

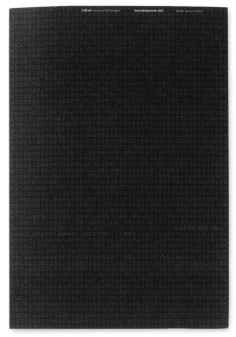

GERMANY

ART DIRECTORS:
GIULIA QUATTROVENTI
MICHAEL LAU

DESIGNER:
MICHAEL LAU

PHOTOGRAPHER:
MICHAEL LAU

CLIENT:
COR AG

SOFTWARE AND
HARDWARE:
QUARKXPRESS
MAC

MATERIALS:
NOBLESSE

PRINTING:
4-COLOR +
4 SPECIALS

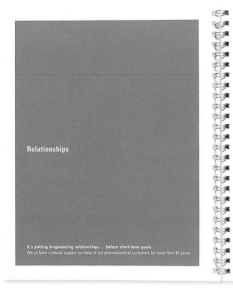

Relationships

It's putting longstanding relationships ... before short-term goals.
We've been a valued supplier to many of our pharmaceutical customers for more than 40 years.

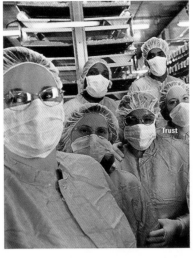

Trust

USA

054
FOSTER DESIGN GROUP
CHARLES RIVER LABORATORIES 2001

ART DIRECTOR:
EDWIN FOSTER

DESIGNER:
RYAN WADE

CLIENT:
CHARLES RIVER
LABORATORIES

PRINTING:
WE ANDREWS 6/6
SHEETFED

What does it take?

Charles River Laboratories

AUSTRALIA

055
CHIMERA DESIGN
DANCEHOUSE ANNUAL REPORT

ART DIRECTOR:
JOHN MAGART

DESIGNER:
NAOMI MACE

CLIENT:
DANCEHOUSE

SOFTWARE:
QUARKXPRESS

MATERIALS:
RALEIGH PAPER

PRINTING:
EMBASSY PRESS

PRODUCT AND SERVICE BROCHURES

CAMPAÑEROS // KO CRÉATION // USINE DE BOUTONS // MADE THOUGHT // FROST DESIGN //
MORLA DESIGN // CAHAN & ASSOCIATES // HAT-TRICK DESIGN // OUT OF THE BLUE //
HEBE. WERBUNG & DESIGN // THE KITCHEN // ATTIK // HAND MADE GROUP // DESIGN5 //
EMERSON, WAJDOWICZ STUDIOS // C375 // PENTAGRAM SF // FAUXPAS // SEA DESIGN // Q //
WILLOUGHBY DESIGN GROUP // NB:STUDIO // MARIUS FAHRNER DESIGN // ROSE DESIGN
ASSOCIATES // BLOK DESIGN // UNA (LONDON) DESIGNERS // FABIO ONGARATO DESIGN //
MUTABOR DESIGN // AJANS ULTRA // HAMBLY & WOOLLEY // IRIDIUM, A DESIGN COMPANY //
DESIGN ASYLUM // EMERY VINCENT DESIGN

:03

GERMANY

/ centrally located / worldwide //

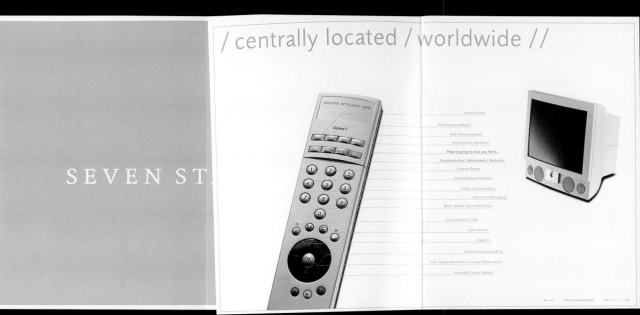

SEVEN ST

ART DIRECTOR:	DESIGNER:	ILLUSTRATOR:	CLIENT:	SOFTWARE AND	PAPER/MATERIAL:
MARTIN KAHRMANN	MARTIN KAHRMANN	MARTIN KAHRMANN	IDF	HARDWARE:	LUXO SANT OFFSET
				QUARKXPRESS	
				MAC	

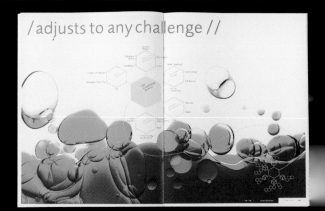

/ adjusts to any challenge //

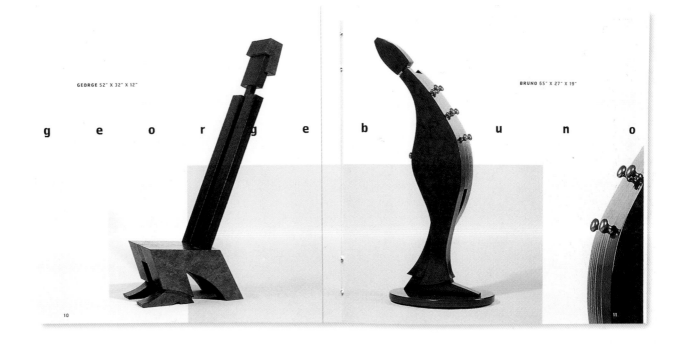

GEORGE 52" X 32" X 12"

g e o r g e b r u n o

BRUNO 65" X 27" X 19"

10

11

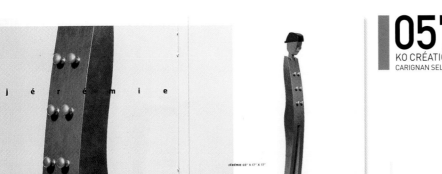

j é r é m i e

JÉRÉMIE 65" X 17" X 17"

06

07

057
KO CRÉATION
CARIGNAN SELF-PROMO

ART DIRECTOR:
ANNIE LACHAPELLE

DESIGNER:
ANNIE LACHAPELLE

CLIENT:
CARIGNAN

SOFTWARE:
QUARKXPRESS

ca ri gna n

ANTOINETTE | ARNO | ARTHUR | BERTA | BRUNO | GEORGE | JÉRÉMIE | JÉRÔMES | XATIA | MERLIN | WILBROD

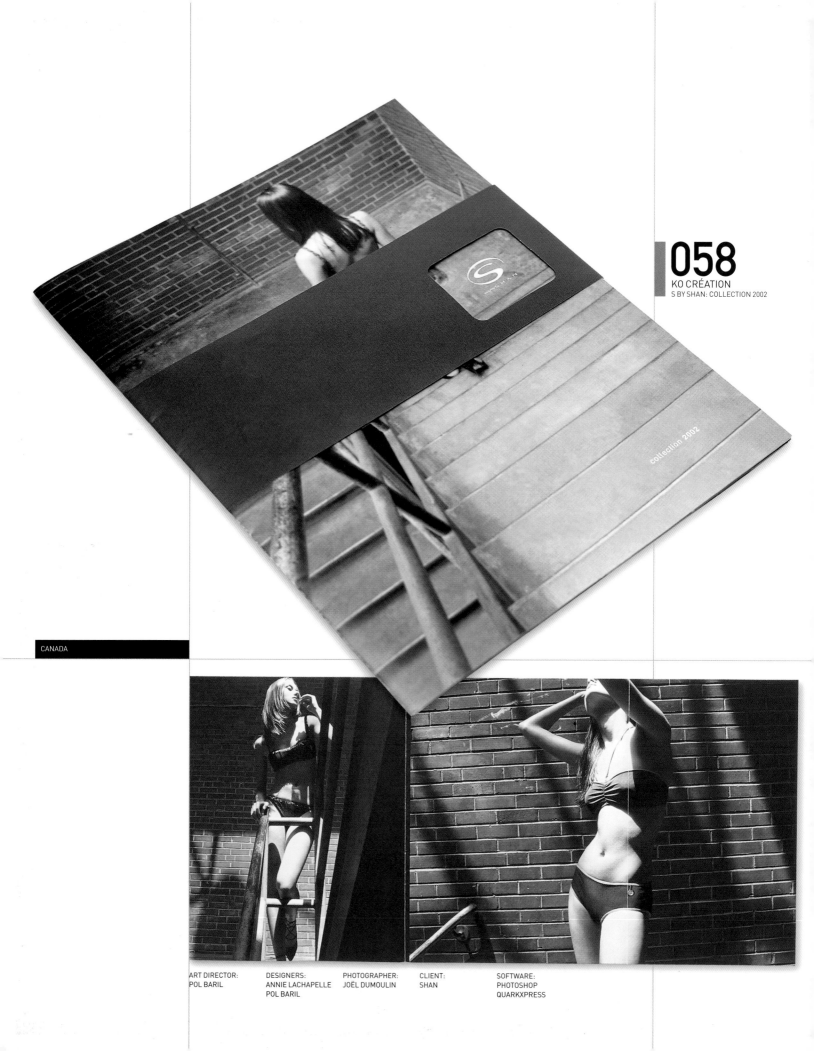

CANADA

ART DIRECTOR:
POL BARIL

DESIGNERS:
ANNIE LACHAPELLE
POL BARIL

PHOTOGRAPHER:
JOËL DUMOULIN

CLIENT:
SHAN

SOFTWARE:
PHOTOSHOP
QUARKXPRESS

059

USINE DE BOUTONS
PIRELLI/DUCATI DFX RACING TEAM

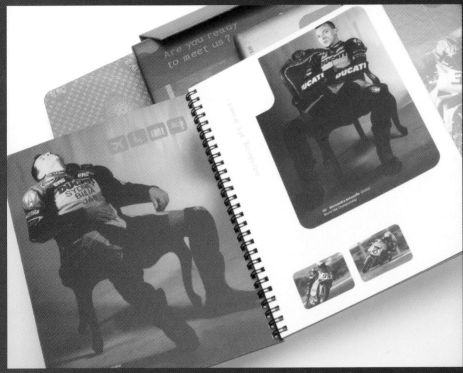

ART DIRECTORS:
LIONELLO BOREAN
CHIARA GRANDESSO

DESIGNER:
LIONELLO BOREAN
CHIARA GRANDESSO

CLIENT:
PIRELLI/DUCATI DFX
RACING TEAM

PRINTING:
CMYK + GOLD

ITALY

ART DIRECTORS:
BEN PARKER
PAUL AUSTIN

DESIGNERS:
BEN PARKER
PAUL AUSTIN

PHOTOGRAPHER:
GEMMA BOOTH

CLIENT:
SONNETI

PRINTING:
PERIVAN

wear
you're
at.®
Spring/Summer 2002 Collections
www.sonneti.com

Sonneti:

UK

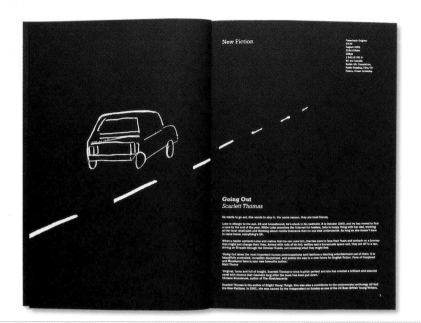

New Fiction

Paperback Original
£6.99
August 2002
216x135mm
256pp
BC dm Canada
Serial, US, Translation,
Radio Reading, Film/TV
Peters, Fraser & Dunlop

Going Out
Scarlett Thomas

He wants to go out. She wants to stay in. For some reason, they are best friends.

UK

ART DIRECTOR:	DESIGNER:	ILLUSTRATOR:	CLIENT:	MATERIALS:	PRINTING:
VINCE FROST	VINCE FROST	MARION DEUCHARS	FOURTH ESTATE	PAPER EPSILON NERO BY FENNER PAPER120GSM + 270GSM	SCREEN PRINTING BY LAUREN DISPLAYS

USA

ART DIRECTOR:	DESIGNERS:	CLIENT:	SOFTWARE:	MATERIALS:	PRINTING:
JENNIFER MORLA	JENNIFER MORLA	WORLD EXPLORER	ILLUSTRATOR	70# LUNA TEXT	GRAPHIC ARTS
	CARRIE FERGUSON	CRUISES	QUARKXPRESS	GLOSS	CENTER

USA

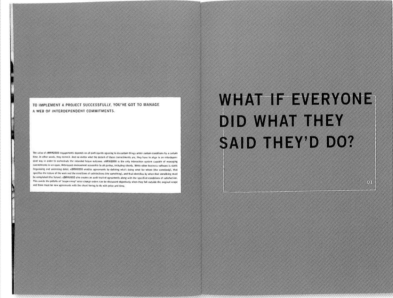

TO IMPLEMENT A PROJECT SUCCESSFULLY, YOU'VE GOT TO MANAGE A WEB OF INTERDEPENDENT COMMITMENTS.

The value of eBRM2000 engagements depends on all participants agreeing to do certain things under certain conditions by a certain time. In other words, they commit. And no matter what the details of these commitments are, they have to align in an interdependent way in order to orchestrate the intended future outcome. eBRM2000 is the only interaction system capable of managing commitments in an open, Web-based environment accessible to all parties, including clients. While other business software is static (legalizing and assessing data), eBRM2000 enables agreements by defining who's doing what for whom (the commitment), that specifies the nature of the work and the conditions of satisfactions (the something), and that identifies by when that something must be completed (the future). eBRM2000 also creates an audit trail of agreements along with the specified conditions of satisfaction. This avoids the pitfalls of "scope-creep" since change orders can be discussed objectively when they fall outside the original scope and there must be new agreements with the client having to do with price and time.

WHAT IF EVERYONE DID WHAT THEY SAID THEY'D DO?

01

80% OF ALL YOUR BUSINESS INTERACTIONS GO UNDOCUMENTED.

ART DIRECTOR:
BILL CAHAN

DESIGNER:
KEVIN ROBERSON

CLIENT:
ACTION TECHNOLOGIES

MATERIALS:
VINTAGE VELVET 80#

PRINTING:
LITHO

DESIGNER:	CLIENT:	SOFTWARE:	MATERIALS:	PRINTING:
HAT-TRICK DESIGN	RABIH HAGE	QUARKXPRESS	COLORPLAN	LITHO & DIE-CUT

065
OUT OF THE BLUE
KEEN BROCHURES

UK

keen

ART DIRECTOR:	DESIGNER:	CLIENT:	SOFTWARE AND	MATERIALS:	PRINTING:
NICK HARPER	NICK HARPER	KEEN GROUP	HARDWARE:	POLYPROP FOLDER	RUSCORBE
		LIMITED	ILLUSTRATOR	250GSM MATT	PRINTING
			PHOTOSHOP	STOCK	
			QUARKXPRESS		
			MAC		

066
HEBE. WERBUNG & DESIGN
MAAS PRODUCT FOLDER

ART DIRECTOR:
REINER HEBE

DESIGNER:
STEFANIE WAHL

ILLUSTRATOR:
DOMINIK ZEHLE

CLIENT:
MAAS GOLDSMITH,
STUTTGART

SOFTWARE AND
HARDWARE:
QUARKXPRESS
MAC

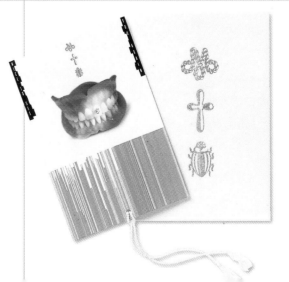

UK

ART DIRECTORS:
ROB PETRIE
PHIL SIMS

Generation
Skye

A3 ▷ A4

25 copies ———————————— to BLAA

▌068
ATTIK
MCNAUGHTON'S PAPER "SKYE"

ART DIRECTOR:
ATTIK

DESIGNER:
ATTIK

PHOTOGRAPHER:
ATTIK

CLIENT:
MCNAUGHTON'S
PAPER

069
HAND MADE GROUP
CORPORATE & PRODUCT CATALOGUES

ART DIRECTOR:	DESIGNER:	PHOTOGRAPHER:	CLIENT:	SOFTWARE AND	MATERIALS:	PRINTING:
ALESSANDRO ESTERI	GIONA MAIARELLI	ALESSANDRO ESTERI	STIMET	HARDWARE:	ZANDERS	OFFSET
			PREFABBRICATI	QUARKXPRESS		
				MAC		

ITALY

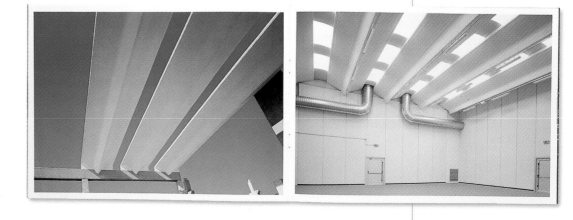

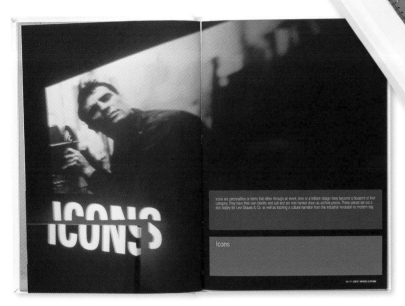

Icons are personalities or items that either through an event, time or a brilliant design have become a blueprint of their category. They have their own identity and cult and are now hunted down as archive pieces. These pieces set out a rich history for Levi Strauss & Co. as well as tracking a cultural narration from the industrial revolution to modern day.

Icons

LEVI'S® VINTAGE CLOTHING SPRING 2001

070
THE KITCHEN
LVC ART BOOK

ART DIRECTORS:
ROB PETRIE
PHIL SIMS

Pop & Protest 15051—0270

Finish: Patchwork

505® Skirt
(1960's)

Based around the 1967 505® jean the long A-line customised skirt was a typical girls silhouette of the early 70's. The 505® jean has a Clean Repair finish in medium blue with stone washing and scraped local abrasion. Made out of denim pieces with different finishes, the skirt is patched together using selvage fabrics, epitomising the style and customisation of garments by youth culture at that time.

1. The famous red ID line of the XX narrow width looms from Cone Mills
2. Bar tacks at pocket corners for extra strength
3. Twin needle Arcuate stitch
4. Zip fly and copper waistband button

USA

ART DIRECTOR:
RON NIKKEL

DESIGNERS:
RACHEL ACTON
CHRIS DUBURG

CLIENT:
TIGÉ BOATS, INC

SOFTWARE AND
HARDWARE:
ILLUSTRATOR
PHOTOSHOP
MAC G4

PRINTING:
GRAPHIC PRESS

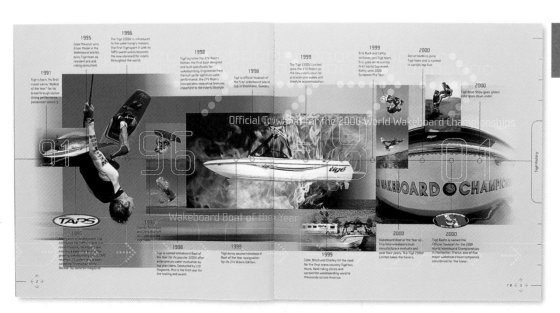

071

DESIGN5
01 BROCHURE

What appears to be is what I deal with.

sn

Sometimes, hum... the scene you p... take a picture of... and it's lifeless, ... you can take a pi... scratching his n... great picture. ☐ I am a professional photographer by trade and an amateur photographer by vocation. Most of the time when I am out of the house I carry a small unobtrusive camera and I snap away obsessively at things that interest me and whatever I think would make a good picture.

USA

museums

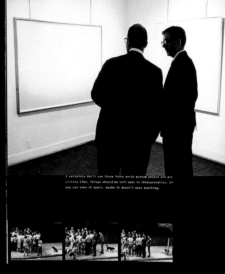

I certainly don't use those funny words museum people and art critics like. Things should be left open to interpretation. If you can take it apart, maybe it doesn't mean anything.

I go to museums to people watch. Because everyone there has gone to look and they are captured in a concentrated place, it is a particularly good thing. For a photographer, rather than fly casting, it's like shooting fish in a barrel. ☐ It is amazing how something which isn't much of anything becomes important when it's framed. Often the frames are more artistic than their contents. They are very reassuring, like the labels. Some people spend more time looking at the labels than at the work itself.

In the end all museums are interesting. Even when they're not.

ART DIRECTORS:
JUREK WAJDOWICZ
LISA LAROCHELLE

DESIGNERS:
JUREK WAJDOWICZ
LISA LAROCHELLE
MANNY MENDEZ

CLIENT:
DOMTAR

SOFTWARE:
QUARKXPRESS

MATERIALS:
BRAVO

PRINTING:
MACDONALD
PRINTING

If my pictures help some people to see things in a certain way, it's probably to look at serious things non-seriously. Everything's serious. Everything's not serious.

073

C375
KREABAGNO BROCHURE

ROMA | *Arte*

Oval biçimli köşe duş tekneleri için tasarlanmış, 2 dışa açılır kapı ve 2 sabit panelden oluşan duş kabini.

Rounded shower enclosure with two pivot doors and two fixed panels for corner shower trays.

ART DIRECTOR:	DESIGNER:	PHOTOGRAPHERS:	CLIENT:	SOFTWARE:	MATERIALS:	PRINTING:
CEM ERUTKU	SEMA DEMIRCIFT	BULENT ERUTKU EMRE IKIZLER	KREABAGNO	FREEHAND PHOTOSHOP	MODO	4-COLOR OFFSET

SIENA | *Arte*

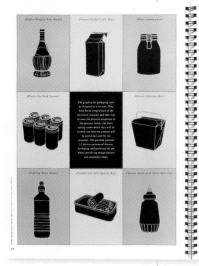

ART DIRECTOR:	DESIGNER:	CLIENT:	SOFTWARE AND HARDWARE:	MATERIALS:	PRINTING:
KIT HINRICHS	MARIA WENZEL	POTLATCH PAPER	ILLUSTRATOR PHOTOSHOP MAC	POTLATCH	ANDERSON, LOS ANGELES

074
PENTAGRAM SF
MCCOY REUNION

USA

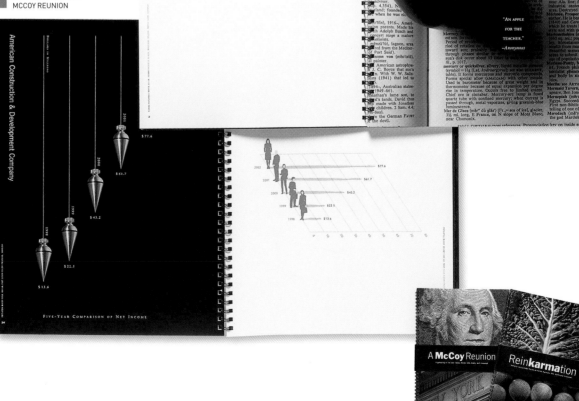

DESIGNERS LOVE OBJECTS RIPE WITH MEANING, AND NO FOOD IS RIPER THAN THE APPLE. IT IS A METAPHOR FOR EVERYTHING FROM ORIGINAL SIN TO THE A-B-CS. ONE REASON THE APPLE FIGURES SO PROMINENTLY IN ADAGES, PROVERBS, AND FOLK LORE IS BECAUSE IT HAS BEEN AROUND SINCE ADAM AND EVE. SOME 7,500 VARIETIES EXIST IN THE WORLD TODAY. A MEMBER OF THE ROSE FAMILY, THE APPLE IS FAMILIAR TO EVERY CULTURE AND LOVED BY PRACTICALLY EVERYONE.

[The Apple]
Food As Metaphor

075
THE KITCHEN
NO BOOK

UK

Michele doesn't wear a zip-front dress, $870, by Yohji Yamamoto.

FREITAG

DECEMBER 2002

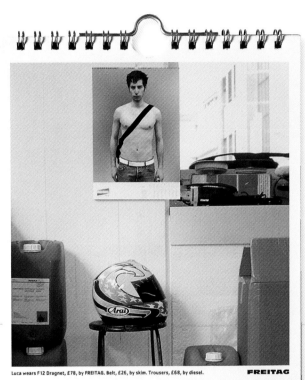

Luca wears F12 Dragnet, £78, by FREITAG. Belt, £26, by skim. Trousers, £68, by diesel.

FREITAG

JANUARY 2002

SWITZERLAND

ART DIRECTOR:	DESIGNER:	FONT DESIGN:	CLIENT:	SOFTWARE AND	MATERIALS:
MARTIN STILLHART	MARTIN STILLHART	MARTIN STILLHART	FREITAG, LTD	HARDWARE: ILLUSTRATOR MAC	BIBER ALLEGRA

076
FAUXPAS
FREITAG CALENDAR 2002

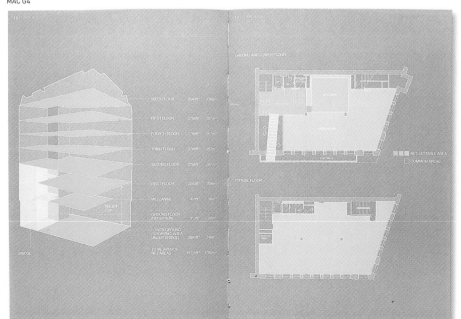

EVEN IN 1925, THE CORNER
OF FARRINGDON ROAD AND
CLERKENWELL ROAD WAS
A PRIME SPOT. TODAY IT'S
A PIVOTAL SPOT.

IT'S WHERE PUBLIC RELATIONS
MEETS PRIVATE BANKING.
WHERE ADVERTISING MEETS
ASSET FINANCE. WHERE THE
MAC MEETS THE PC.

AS SUCH, IT WOULD SUIT A
LEGAL OR FINANCIAL COMPANY
MOVING WEST. OR A CREATIVE
COMPANY MOVING EAST.

077
SEA DESIGN
THE CORNER

UK

ART DIRECTOR:	DESIGNER:	CLIENT:	SOFTWARE AND	MATERIALS:	PRINTING:
JOHN SIMPSON	JAMIE ROBERTS	PILCHER HERSHAM	HARDWARE:	NATURALIS	4-COLOR +
			ILLUSTRATOR	GALLERY SILK	EMBOSSING
			PHOTOSHOP	ARTIC WHITE	
			QUARKXPRESS	SMOOTH	
			MAC G4		

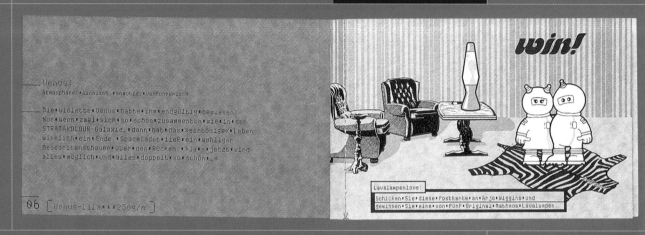

078
Q
MISSION STRATAKOLOUR

ART DIRECTOR:
THILO VON
DEBSCHITZ

DESIGNER:
MATTHIAS FREY

PHOTOGRAPHER:
MATTHIAS FREY

CLIENT:
ARJO WIGGINS
GERMANY

SOFTWARE AND
HARDWARE:
ILLUSTRATOR
QUARKXPRESS
MAC

MATERIALS:
STRATAKOLOUR

PRINTING:
GORIUS DRUCK &
SERVICE

ART DIRECTOR:	DESIGNER:	CLIENT:	SOFTWARE AND	MATERIALS:	PRINTING:
ANN WILLOUGHBY	TRENTON KENAGY	EL DORADO INC	HARDWARE:	UNCOATED	IN-HOUSE
			QUARKXPRESS	CHIPBOARD	
			MAC		

USA

079
WILLOUGHBY DESIGN GROUP
BARN BOOK

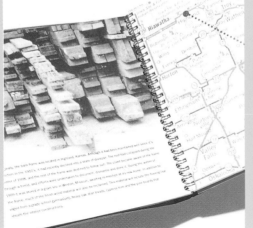

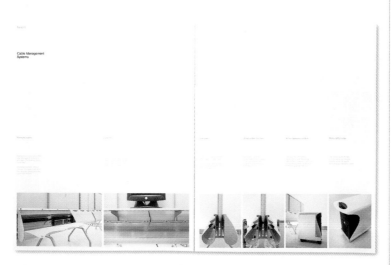

080
SEA DESIGN
BEYON

ART DIRECTOR:
BRYAN EDMONDSON

CLIENT:
RICHMOND
SOLUTIONS

SOFTWARE AND
HARDWARE:
ILLUSTRATOR
PHOTOSHOP
QUARKXPRESS
MAC G4

MATERIALS:
GALLERY ART SILK
170GSM

PRINTING:
CASE BOUND +
EMBOSS + 4-COLOR
+ M/C VARNISH

UK

ART DIRECTORS:
ALAN DYE
NICK FINNEY
BEN STOTT

DESIGNER:
NICK VINCENT

CLIENT:
PENGUIN
PUBLISHING

SOFTWARE:
QUARKXPRESS

MATERIALS:
COVER: FENNER
CONSTRUCTION
CHARCOAL
BOUNDED WITH
SUEDAL LUX;
TEXT: 200GSM SILK
TRACE: T2000,
CHAPTERS: MEAD
CUSTOM KOTE

PRINTING:
ETHEDO PRESS

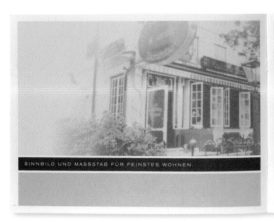

ART DIRECTORS: DESIGNERS: CLIENT: SOFTWARE: MATERIALS: PRINTING:
MARIUS FAHRNER   MARIUS FAHRNER   DAHLER & COMPANY   FREEHAND   RÖMERTURM   4-COLOR OFFSET
UMUB ETTERLIG   UMUB ETTERLIG   PROJECT MARKETING   CURTIS ESPARTO

|082
MARIUS FAHRNER DESIGN
AVANTGARDE

GERMANY

westzone°
new angles on life

preview° Spring 2001

083
ROSE DESIGN ASSOCIATES, LTD
WESTZONE AUTUMN CATALOG

Afghanistan

The ageless rhythms of daily life
in Afghanistan's fields, villages
and towns are disrupted by war,
displacement and natural disaster.

| UK/US Con | Published | 303 x 230mm | 9¾ x 10¾" | 128pp | 75 duotone | Hardcover | 1903391 13 X |
| £30/\$60/\$75 | | | | | | | |

The Divine Frenzy:
Ritual and Possession
in Hindu Kerala
Pepita Seth

Illuminating photographs and texts
chart the way in which the people
of this region of southern India fuse
with their land and their gods.

| UK/US Con | Published | 309 x 245mm | 9¾ x 13" | 208pp | 140 colour | Hardcover | 1903391 14 8 |
| £30/\$65/\$75 | | | | | | | |

Stones: The Megaliths of
England & Wales and the
Stories Behind Them
David and Lai Ngan Corio

Stunning photography is accompanied
by the fascinating variety of literature,
opinions and fantasies inspired by the
presence of ancient stones on the
British landscape.

| UK/US Con | Published | 254 x 254mm | 10 x 10" | 160pp | 64 duotone | Hardcover | 1903391 15 6 |
| £30/\$60/\$75 | | | | | | | |

Carving the Mountains:
The Marble Quarries of Carrara
Guido Buffoni and Stephen Cox

Guido Buffoni has photographed
the marble quarries of northern
Italy since the 1970s. His images
are accompanied by an overview
of Carrara's history by British
sculptor Stephen Cox.

| UK/US Con | April 2001 | 360 x 360mm | 12 x 12" | 160pp | 120 colour + b/w | Hardcover | 1903391 22 9 |
| £40/\$85/\$100 | | | | | | | |

Fuck Off Typography
Various
Edited by Gerard Saint

Rush

Londoners love and hate their home in equal measure. Not that they would demonstrate such strong emotions in public – such things are best left to the hot-heads of New York, Paris or Rome. Instead they set their city faces hard and walk apart, though with the herd. Occasionally they will let their hair down – at New Year's Eve, for example. Momentarily, they may give vent to their frustration at missing a bus or losing a purse. But before long it's back to the routine, as if nothing ever happened, dreaming personal island dreams as the herd returns to graze.

Photographer Jocelyn Bain Hogg has teamed up with award-winning poet Neil Rollinson to explore the 21st-century London experience, from the remnants of Empire to 'Cool Britannia' chic, from the chaos of a groaning public transport system to moments of tranquility in the city's parks and gardens.

Author

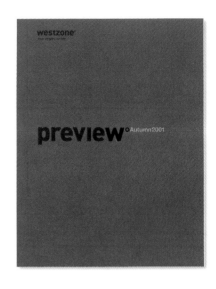

ART DIRECTOR:
SIMON ELLIOTT

DESIGNER:
SIMON ELLIOTT

CLIENT:
WESTZONE
PUBLISHING, LTD

SOFTWARE:
ILLUSTRATOR
PHOTOSHOP
QUARKXPRESS

MATERIALS:
VALLIANT SATIN ART

PRINTING:
OFFSET LITHO

Fuck Off Typography
Various
Edited by Gerard Saint

Publication
June

Cover price
£40

Format
330mm x 265mm

Page extent
176

Illustrations
124 colour +
b/w plates

Cover
Hardcover

ISBN
1 903391 21 0

Title
Fuck Off Typography invites prolific typographers, graphic designers and illustrators from the UK and international scene to trade visual insults. Peppered with expletives, *Fuck Off Typography* explores and offers insight into obscure taboo colloquialisms, and explores the creation of brand new, sharp-witted profanities expressed through the medium of typography.

Contributors include Paul Davis, Jasper Goodall, Dave Foldvari, Michael Gillette, Christophe Gowans, London design companies Form, Monster and many others, alongside their illustrious international contemporaries.

Author
Gerard Saint is an art director and co-founder of the London design group Big-Active.

ART DIRECTOR:
VANESSA ECKSTEIN

DESIGNERS:
VANESSA ECKSTEIN
FRANCES CHEN

CLIENT:
NIENKAMPER

SOFTWARE:
ILLUSTRATOR

MATERIALS:
BECKETT

PRINTING:
LITHO

CANADA

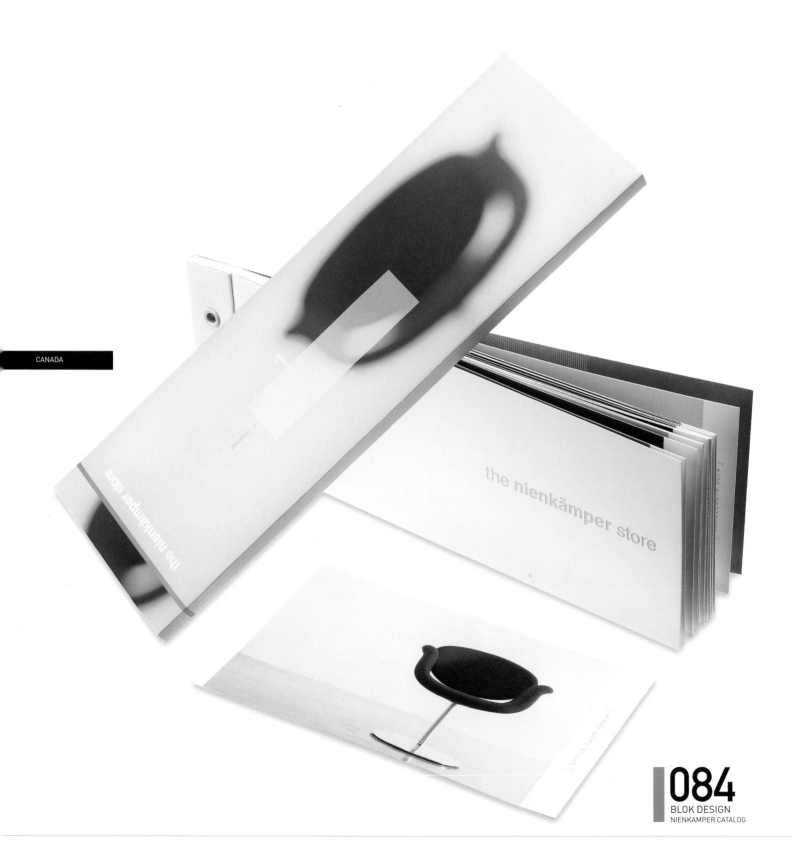

the nienkämper store

the nienkämper store

DAHLER & COMPANY
PROJEKTMARKETING

JEDER BAUGRUND BIRGT EIN POTENZIAL

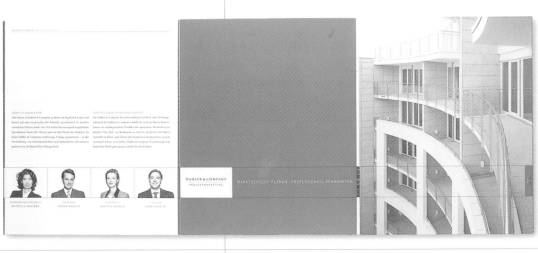

Dahler & Company GmbH

Seit Jahren ist Dahler & Company zu Hause in begehrten Lagen und damit auf eine anspruchsvolle Klientel spezialisiert. In perfekt vernetzten Händen durch vor die reibt beansprucht ausgebildeten Spezialisten-Teams der Wünsch ganz in den Dienst des Kunden. So kann Dahler & Company erstklassige Erfolge garantieren – in der Vermittlung von Wohnimmobilien und Immobilien-Investoren genauso wie im Immobilien-Management.

Dahler & Company Projektmarketing GmbH

Die Dahler & Company Projektmarketing GmbH ist eine Tochtergesellschaft der Dahler & Company GmbH. Sie weiß aus Ihrer Bauerfahren ein marktgerechtes Produkt und optimalen Mieteinfluss zu machen. Das Ziel: von Startegien so viel wie möglich vom Bauträger verkauft zu haben und durch alle Bauphasen hindurch die zweite optimalen Preise zu erzielen. Dahler & Company Projektmarketing leistet dazu Markt ganz. Lernen Sie uns kennen.

DAHLER & COMPANY
PROJEKTMARKETING

MARKTGERECHT PLANEN - PROFESSIONELL VERMARKTEN

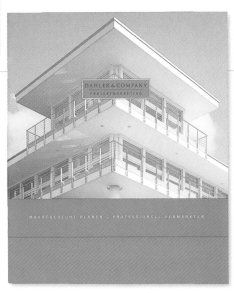

DAHLER & COMPANY
PROJEKTMARKETING

MARKTGERECHT PLANEN - PROFESSIONELL VERMARKTEN

ART DIRECTOR:	DESIGNER:	CLIENT:	SOFTWARE:	MATERIALS:	PRINTING:
MARIUS FAHRNER DESIGN	MARIUS FAHRNER DESIGN	DAHLER & COMPANY PROJECT MARKETING	FREEHAND	250GSM AMBITION	2-COLOR OFFSET

ART DIRECTOR:	DESIGNER:	CLIENT:	SOFTWARE AND	MATERIALS:	PRINTING:
NICK BELL	AXEL FELDMANN	PETER MILNE	HARDWARE:	FEDRIGONI SAVILLE	PAUL GREEN
		FURNITURE MAKERS	QUARKXPRESS	ROW + FEDRIGONI	PRINTING [LITHO]
			MAC	DALI NEVE + B&C	
				GALERIE ART GLOSS	

086
UNA (LONDON) DESIGNERS
PETER MILNE FURNITURE MAKERS

Laurence King Publishing
Autumn 2001

UK

ART DIRECTOR:	DESIGNERS:	CLIENT:	MATERIALS:	PRINTING:
VINCE FROST	VINCE FROST	LAURENCE KING	NEW FORMATION	PRINCIPAL COLOR
	SONYA DYAKOVA	PUBLISHING LTD	SUPERFINE 100GSM	(LITHO)

Laurence King Publishing
World Rights 2002

088
FABIO ONGARATO DESIGN
EXPRESSION PAPER PROMO

AUSTRALIA

ART DIRECTOR:	DESIGNER:	PHOTOGRAPHER:	CLIENT:	MATERIALS:	PRINTING:
FABIO ONGARATO	YARRA LAURIE	DEREK HENDERSON	K. W. DOGGETT	EXPRESSION	GUNN & TAYLOR

ART DIRECTOR:
JOHANNES PLASS

DESIGNER:
KRISTINA
DULLMANN

PHOTOGRAPHER:
CARSTEN RAFFEL

CLIENT:
SINNER SCHRADER

MATERIALS:
ZANDERS MEDLEY
PURE

PRINTING:
DRUCKGEREI
BRÜNNER

089
MUTABOR DESIGN
SINNER SCHRADER RECRUITING FLYER

GERMANY

ART DIRECTOR:
NAZLI ONGAN

DESIGNER:
NAZLI ONGAN

PHOTOGRAPHER:
ABDULLAH
HEKIMHAN

CLIENT:
VAKKO

SOFTWARE:
FREEHAND

MATERIALS:
NONBRILLIANT
GLAZED PAPER

PRINTING:
4-COLOR OFFSET

Home networking:
Smarter the second time around

JACQUES BUGHIN, RENÉ FOSTER, ALAN MILES, LUIS UBIÑAS, MATTHIAS WINTER

A fanciful first attempt at the networked home has given way to a more sensible model with robust demand and positive economics. While takeup rates will vary between Europe and North America, networking services could become vital competitive stakes in the battle to own the home.

F2 Overview

100 million users can't be wrong:
Competitive insights for a broadband world

SCOTT BEARDSLEY, JOE BERCHTOLD, JEFF KARISH, WILHELM ROHN, LUIS UBIÑAS

ART DIRECTOR:	DESIGNER:	CLIENT:	
BARB WOOLLEY	DOMINIC AYRE	MCKINSEY & COMPANY	CANADA

future
intelligence 2
f2

Broadband's Quiet Revolution
Opportunities and Outlooks

Since its inception, broadband has quietly, steadily rolled out to over 100 million users around the world. What happens next, in the battle to profit from access and applications, won't be quiet at all.

McKinsey&Company

RESOURCES. KNOWLEDGE. DEADLINES.

FAX. 416 599 9829   TEL. 416 599 1847
49 spadina avenue suite 506

FROM

IDEA GENERATION TO PROJECT AND CAMPAIGN
MANAGEMENT AND BEYOND. WE ARE A UNIQUE
PRODUCTION RESOURCE, CONSISTENTLY DE-
LIVERING THE BEST CONTACTS, PRICE LEVERAGE,
SYSTEMS, PROCEDURES, AND LIAISON SERVICES.
WE TAKE PRIDE IN OUR ABILITY TO MEET EVERY
DEADLINE, AND IN THE CREATIVITY AND KNOW-
LEDGE WE BRING TO EVERY ASSIGNMENT.

ART DIRECTOR:
VANESSA ECKSTEIN

DESIGNERS:
VANESSA ECKSTEIN
FRANCES CHEN

CLIENT:
THE PRODUCTION
KITCHEN

MATERIALS:
BENEFIT

PRINTING:
SOMERSET
GRAPHICS

CANADA

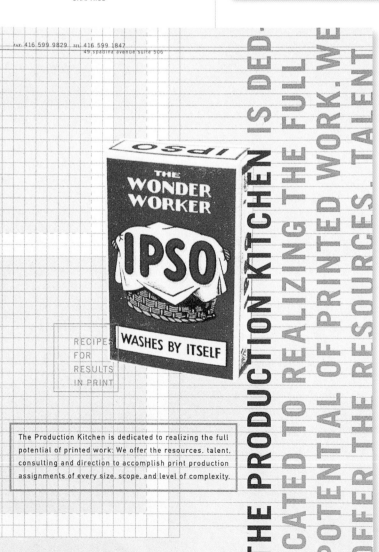

THE
WONDER
WORKER

IPSO

WASHES BY ITSELF

RECIPES
FOR
RESULTS
IN PRINT

The Production Kitchen is dedicated to realizing the full
potential of printed work. We offer the resources, talent,
consulting and direction to accomplish print production
assignments of every size, scope, and level of complexity.

092
BLOK DESIGN
THE PRODUCTION KITCHEN
SALES KIT

ART DIRECTOR:
MARTIN STILLHART

DESIGNER:
MARTIN STILLHART

CLIENT:
SKIM.COM

SOFTWARE:
ILLUSTRATOR
QUARKXPRESS

MATERIALS:
INVERCOAT 240GSM

PRINTING:
OFFSET

SWITZERLAND

093
FAUXPAS
LEPORELLO

Our Vision

We are changing the way you communicate. We bring together video, voice and data over your IP, ATM or SONET network to enable interactive video communications and real-time video transport. Crystal clear video. Pure audio with exceptionally low delay. Flexible solutions to fit the way you work. With the quality of technologies like MPEG-2, and the reliability of a dedicated platform, Miranda Media Networks truly brings you **face to face**.

Changing the
Face of
Communication

Teach

Video expands the reach of educators and the ability of students to learn. With MPEG-2 technology from Miranda Media Networks, universities, schools, and professional colleges are using their resources more effectively. Video networks tie together statewide school systems, giving students better access to unique classes and greater flexibility in course schedules. Educators have access to best-in-class speakers who are no longer limited by geography or flight availability. Education is about expanding knowledge, and high quality video can provide the connectivity to make it happen.

Empowering
Distance
Learning

Live

The difference is quality. Medicine is a world of images, and their accuracy can mean life or death. Reliable, interactive MPEG-2 video enables doctors and specialists to learn, diagnose and treat today's patients more accurately and effectively. And video has become an invaluable part of the critically important teaching process for medical students and interns. In short - video communications can bring the knowledge of experts to those who need it.

Making a
Difference in
Diagnosis

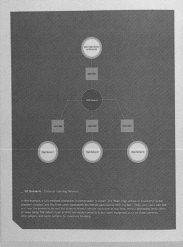

CANADA

ART DIRECTOR: MARIO L'ÉCUYER	DESIGNER: JEAN-FRANÇOIS PLANTE	PHOTOGRAPHER: HEADLIGHT INNOVATIVE IMAGERY	CLIENT: MIRANDA MEDIA NETWORKS	SOFTWARE AND HARDWARE: ILLUSTRATOR PHOTOSHOP QUARKXPRESS MAC 7500	MATERIALS: EUROART SILK	PRINTING: BEAUREGARD PRINTERS

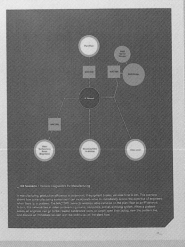

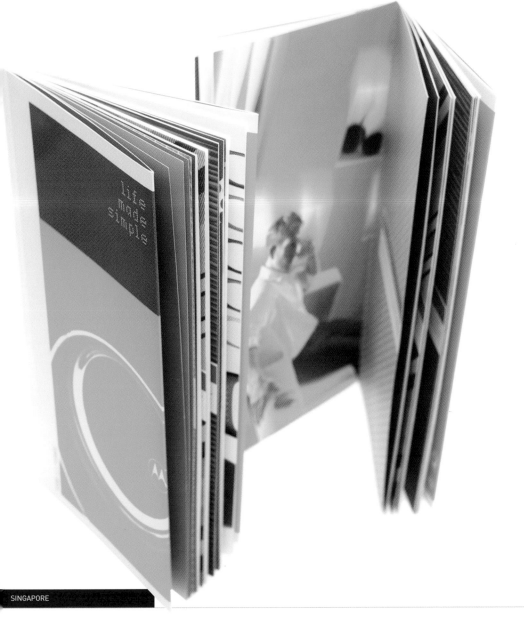

life
made
simple

SINGAPORE

ART DIRECTOR:
CHRISTOPHER LEE

DESIGNERS:
CHRISTOPHER LEE
CARA ANG

CLIENT:
MOTOROLA
ELECTRONICS
PTE LTD

SOFTWARE:
FREEHAND

MATERIALS:
MATT ARTPAPER

PRINTING:
4C X 4C

Think business
lunches. Rubbing
shoulders with
corporate
powers. Think
glamorous
parties, and
mingling with the
chic and well-
heeled. Think
Silicon Valley
at the altars
of worshipping
technophiles.
Think family
and loved ones.
Whatever your
needs may be,
Motorola has a
world of wireless
communications
devices to
simplify your life.

Zukunftsmarkt Mobilität

Eine Studie von Trendbüro im Auftrag von RMS

>> NO LIMITS <<

R·M·S Radio Marketing Service

Mobilität & Gesellschaft

1. Sozialer Wandel
2. Technologischer Wandel
3. Ökonomischer Wandel
4. Kultureller Wandel

Ein Kickboard allein macht noch keinen Trend. Ein gesellschaftlicher Wandel vollzieht sich nicht auf einer einzigen Ebene. Erst wenn wir den Roller in Zusammenhang mit den gewachsenen Mobilitäts- und Flexibilitätsansprüchen einer multimedialen Gesellschaft sehen, wenn wir beobachten, wie die Bereitschaft zum berufsbedingten Umzug ebenso wie die Verkehrsrate steigt und mehr als jeder zweite Deutsche ein Handy und ein Auto besitzt, sprechen wir von einem gesellschaftlichen Wertewandel.

Im ersten Teil lesen Sie, wie sich Mobilität auf der sozialen Ebene und auf das private Umfeld auswirkt – wenn nötig per SMS. So erlaubt die britische Stadt Liverpool nun ihren Bürgern als erste Wahlbehörde, ihre Stimmen zur Kommunalwahl auch per SMS, Telefon oder Internet abzugeben.

Im technologischen Wandel wird beschrieben, wie IT-Technologie hilft, Bewegungsfreiheit zu schaffen, zum Beispiel in einer Stadt wie London, in der sich die Durchschnittsgeschwindigkeit von heute nicht von der des Postkutschenzeitalters von vorgestern unterscheidet. Laut International Association of Public Transport liegt sie im Zentrum Londons bei 16 km/h.

Wie man aus Zeit ein Geschäft macht, erfahren Sie beim ökonomischen Wandel. Businessnomaden, Teleworker und E-Lancer verlangen nach neuen Angeboten – wie etwa Coffee to go – der in Coffeeshops im amerikanischen Stil und beim Bäcker mittlerweile an jeder Ecke zu haben ist.

Der kulturelle Wandel schließlich zeigt, warum Sneakers – vom 70er-Jahre-Treter bis zum Hightech-Turnschuh 2002 – einen solchen Boom erleben, warum sie den Nerv unserer Zeit treffen und wie allgemein eine Versportung auf ästhetischer Ebene festzustellen ist.

04/05

| 096 |
| CAMPAÑEROS |
| RMS TRENDSTUDIE MOBILITY |

ART DIRECTORS:
GIULIA QUATTROVENTI
MICHAEL LAU

DESIGNER:
MICHAEL LAU

PHOTOGRAPHER:
PATRIZIA PIEPRYZK

CLIENT:
RADIO MARKETING
SERVICE

SOFTWARE AND
HARDWARE:
QUARKXPRESS
MAC

MATERIALS:
PHOENOMATT

PRINTING:
4-COLOR + 1 SPOT
COLOR

ART DIRECTOR:
EMERY VINCENT
DESIGN

DESIGNER:
EMERY VINCENT
DESIGN

CLIENT:
MACQUARIE FUNDS
MANAGEMENT

AUSTRALIA

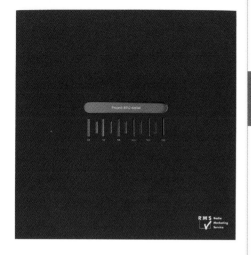

GERMANY

ART DIRECTOR:	DESIGNER:	CLIENT:	SOFTWARE AND	MATERIALS:	PRINTING:
PATRIZIA PIEPRYZK	PATRIZIA PIEPRYZK	RADIO MARKETING SERVICE	HARDWARE: QUARKXPRESS MAC	DUOCARD PROFISTAR	4-COLOR + 1 SPOT COLOR

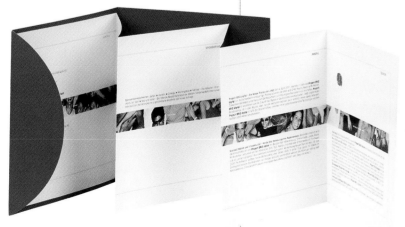

GERMANY

099
CAMPAÑEROS
LEITZ IMAGE BROCHURE

Das sind ja schöne Aussichten.
+49 (0)180/3 22 33 50
A bright prospect!

ART DIRECTOR:	DESIGNER:	PHOTOGRAPHER:	CLIENT:	SOFTWARE AND HARDWARE:	MATERIALS:	PRINTING:
MARTIN KAHRMANN	MARTIN KAHRMANN	MARTIN KAHRMANN	ESSELTE LEITZ INDIVIDUAL	QUARKXPRESS MAC	PHOENOMATT	4-COLOR + 2 SPOT COLOR

Bei uns können Sie sich einige Freiheiten erlauben.
Your individuality is okay with us.

NON-PROFIT, EDUCATIONAL, INSTITU
AND HEALTHCARE BROCHURES

ATTIK // ORIGIN // RADLEY YELDAR // POULIN + MORRIS // CLARK CREATIVE GROUP // CHENG
DESIGN // WILLIAM HOMAN DESIGN // UNA (LONDON) DESIGNERS // EMERY VINCENT DESIGN //
IRIDIUM, A DESIGN AGENCY // ENERGY ENERGY DESIGN // 2D3D // NBBJ GRAPHIC DESIGN //
CHEN DESIGN ASSOCIATES // MARIUS FAHRNER DESIGN // FORM // USINE DE BOUTONS //
THIRTEEN DESIGN // BOSTOCK & POLLITT // MADE THOUGHT

TIONAL,

To stop all
cruelty
to children
FULL Stop

University of
HUDDERSFIELD

NSPCC

To stop all
cruelty
to c

NSPCC

:04

ART DIRECTOR:
ATTIK

DESIGNER:
ATTIK

PHOTOGRAPHER:
ATTIK

CLIENT:
UNIVERSITY OF
HUDDERSFIELD

100
ATTIK
UNIVERSITY OF HUDDERSFIELD

101
ORIGIN
NCBS BROCHURE

The National Centre for Business & ...
(NCBS) is a sustainable solutions ...
This means that environmental protection ...
social responsibility are at the heart of ...
company's business activities.

We are committed to helping individuals and ...
organisations minimise the environmental and ...
social impacts of their activities, and because ...
we believe in practising what we preach, we ...
will endeavour to minimise those impacts arising ...
from our own activities.

DESIGN DIRECTOR:	DESIGNER:	CLIENT:	PAPER/MATERIAL:	PRINTING:
MARK BOTTOMLEY	ADAM LEE	NCBS	PULP BOARD	DEBOSSED TYPE

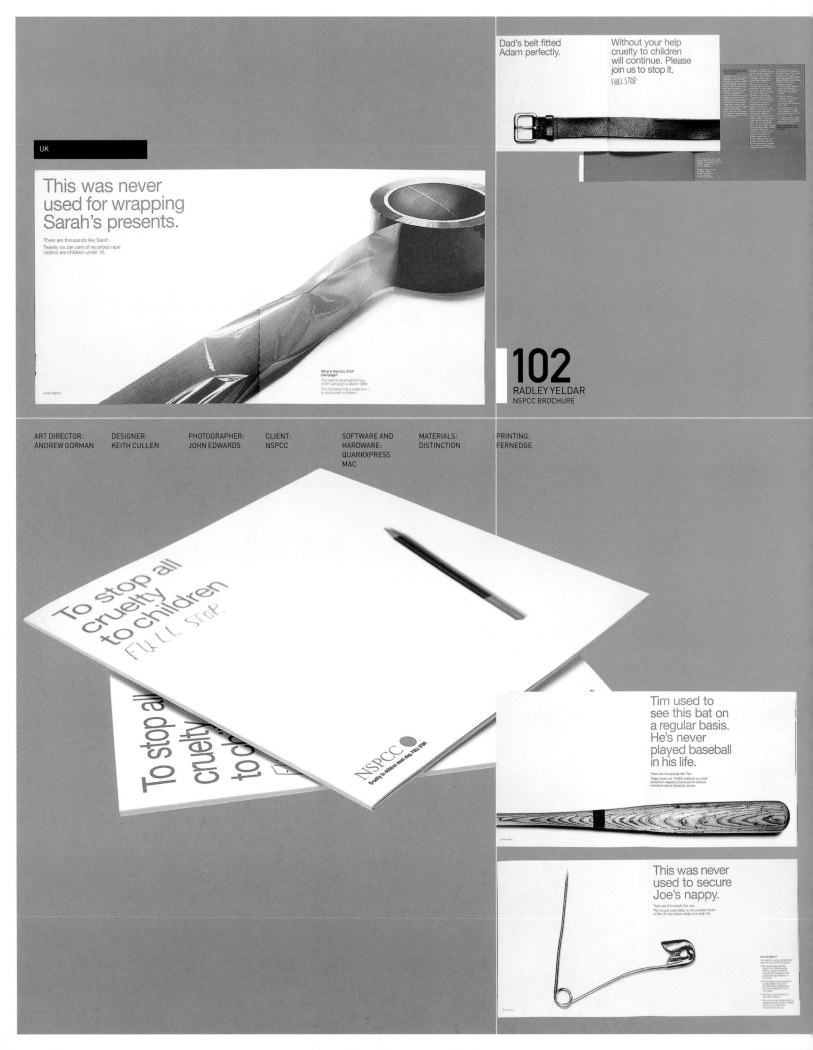

UK

This was never
used for wrapping
Sarah's presents.

There are thousands like Sarah.
Twenty six per cent of recorded rape
victims are children under 16.

What is the FULL STOP
Campaign?
The NSPCC launched the FULL
STOP Campaign in March 1999.
The Campaign has a single aim —
to end cruelty to children.

Dad's belt fitted
Adam perfectly.

Without your help
cruelty to children
will continue. Please
join us to stop it.
FULL STOP

102
RADLEY YELDAR
NSPCC BROCHURE

ART DIRECTOR:
ANDREW GORMAN

DESIGNER:
KEITH CULLEN

PHOTOGRAPHER:
JOHN EDWARDS

CLIENT:
NSPCC

SOFTWARE AND
HARDWARE:
QUARKXPRESS
MAC

MATERIALS:
DISTINCTION

PRINTING:
FERNEDGE

To stop all
cruelty
to children
FULL STOP.

NSPCC
Cruelty to children must stop FULL STOP

Tim used to
see this bat on
a regular basis.
He's never
played baseball
in his life.

There are thousands like Tim.
Today there are 10,000 children on child
protection registers because of serious
concerns about physical abuse.

This was never
used to secure
Joe's nappy.

There are thousands like Joe.
The cruelty most likely to a violent death
in the UK are babies under one year old.

103
POULIN + MORRIS
YALE UNIVERSITY: A FRAMEWORK
FOR CAMPUS

ART DIRECTOR:
L RICHARD POULIN

DESIGNER:
AMY KWON

CLIENT:
COOPER,
ROBERTSON &
PARTNERS

SOFTWARE:
QUARKXPRESS

MATERIALS:
MOHAWK
SUPERFINE

PRINTING:
UNIVERSAL
PRINTING

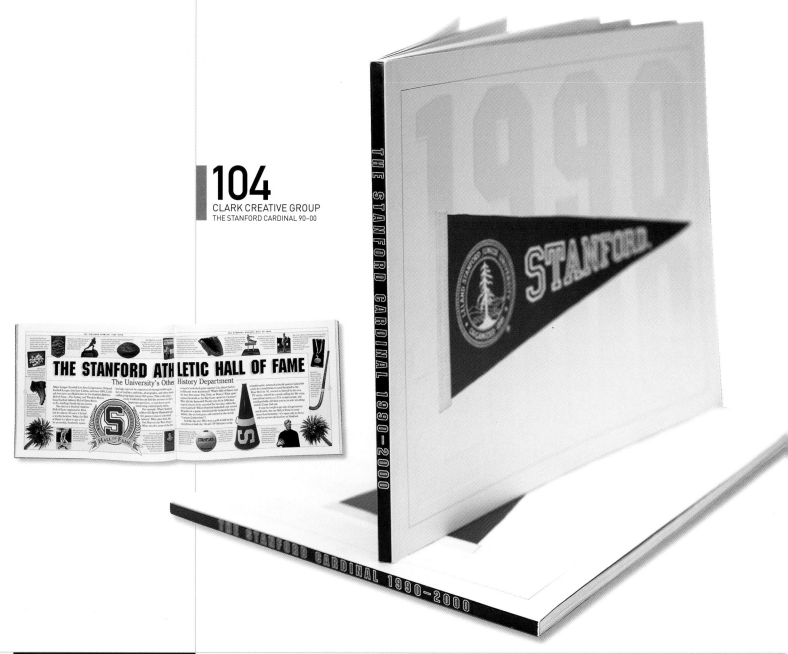

104
CLARK CREATIVE GROUP
THE STANFORD CARDINAL 90–00

ART DIRECTOR:	DESIGNER:	CLIENT:	SOFTWARE:	MATERIALS:	PRINTING:
ANNEMARIE CLARK	NOREEN REI FUKUMORI	STANFORD ATHLETIC DEPT	ILLUSTRATOR PHOTOSHOP QUARKXPRESS	CENTURA	HEMLOCK PRINTERS

Sponsored by Seattle Arts & Lectures and the Simpson Center for the Humanities

2000-01

SEMINARS IN THE HUMANITIES FOR K-12 TEACHERS

1 The Odyssey: History, Transmission, and Performance

2 Contemporary Women Writers and Stories of Emotion

3 Doing More than Watching: Big Brother Today

4 John Singer Sargent and the Triumph and Collapse of Portraiture

5 Love as Theatre: The Drama of Shakespeare's Sonnets

6 Information, Anxiety, and the K-12 Classroom

7 That's My Song! Popular Music and American Culture

8 Beowulf: Medieval Heroes and Monsters in the Modern World

9 What is China?

10 The Information Democracy

as

teachers
SCHOLARS

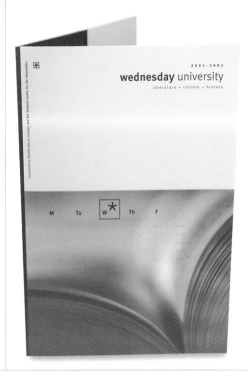

2001-2002

wednesday university
literature • culture • history

M   Tu   W   Th   F

DESIGNER:
KAREN CHENG

CLIENT:
SEATTLE ARTS
AND LECTURES

SOFTWARE:
ILLUSTRATOR
PHOTOSHOP
QUARKXPRESS

MATERIALS:
FINCH FINE
COVER + TEXT

PRINTING:
2 PMS COLORS

USA

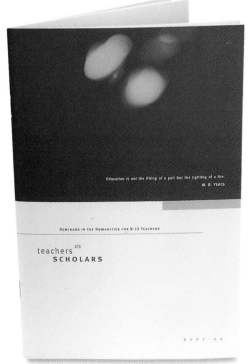

Education is not the filling of a pail but the lighting of a fire.
W. B. YEATS

SEMINARS IN THE HUMANITIES FOR K-12 TEACHERS

teachers *as*
SCHOLARS

Mission Guadalupe Alternative Programs fosters learning, personal growth and skill development in those individuals who are not well served by mainstream educational institutions.

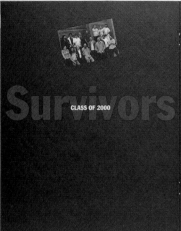

Survivors

CLASS OF 2000

Imagine attending high school while you are pregnant or getting yourself and your child ready for school every morning. Imagine arriving in this country as a teenager and having to learn a second language while taking academic courses required for graduation. Imagine getting a year or more behind your class-mates in school, but persevering and graduating anyway. Imagine the pressure and honor of being the first person in your family to graduate.
The 23 students who made up the GAP graduating class of 2000 have lived through situations that some of us can only imagine. They are a group of survivors and left high school just a few weeks ago as seasoned, confident young adults ready to seize their futures. To a person, they know how to set and achieve goals, use their resources, help one another. They are ready. In their words, GAP has been a small place where they got individual attention, where teachers were cool, and where students got along well together. It is a nice thing to think about now that they are gone and we look forward to the beginning of another school year.

ART DIRECTOR:
WILLIAM HOMAN

DESIGNER:
WILLIAM HOMAN

CLIENT:
GUADALUPE
ALTERNATIVE
PROGRAM

MATERIALS:
CLASSIC CREST

PRINTING:
CUSTOM COLOR
PRINTING

106

WILLIAM HOMAN DESIGN
GUADALUPE ALTERNATIVE PROGRAM

Milestones of the millennium As we move forward into the next century, our goal is to be prepared to meet the needs of all current and future GAP students. We have grown from a one-room house to a building with programs that provide multiple educational opportunities for youth and adults. **We** have reached many milestones this year. On an academic level, our students' scores improved substantially over last year. Culturally, through collaborations and partnerships, students have learned about the richness and diversity of others, the importance of tradition and the need to respect each other. They continue to prepare for the technological advances of the future and the need for communication and computer skills. **We** can achieve these goals because of the commitment and dedication of the staff. Congratulations to Sister Anna Louise Wilson, who will be celebrating her fiftieth anniversary as a School Sister of Notre Dame. She has worked at GAP for 25 years. Her contributions to GAP have been legendary. She has received numerous awards, but what is more important to her is the contact she makes with students in her art classes. **The** board has diligently worked this year to provide the resources for staff members to create an environment that allows each student to reach his or her potential. A new strategic plan has been adopted to position us for the future. We remain committed to the mission of GAP. Karen Thompson, Chair, GAP Board of Directors

Sister Ann

This annual report reviews the year 1999 and, we hope, shows that this agency is secure financially and solid as an educational institution—as it always has been. It also celebrates the graduating class of 2000 and the teachers and support staff who had so much to do with the success of our new-century graduates. We appreciate them and their talents and we also, and in the same breath, appreciate you and your support of GAP. In a unique way, your dedication to our mission is felt here every day, helping us create a place where learning and opportunity are realities.

Thanks

UK

ART DIRECTOR:
NICK BELL

DESIGNER:
AXEL FELDMANN

PHOTOGRAPHER:
JANERIK POSTH

CLIENT:
LONDON COLLEGE
OF PRINTING

SOFTWARE AND
HARDWARE:
QUARKXPRESS
MAC

MATERIALS:
TUCKY WOODFREE
MATT ART

PRINTING:
SOUTH SEA
INTERNATIONAL
PRESS LTD

AUSTRALIA

ART DIRECTOR:
EMERY VINCENT
DESIGN

DESIGNER:
EMERY VINCENT
DESIGN

CLIENT:
UTS

108
EMERY VINCENT DESIGN
CAREERS & COURSES GUIDE 2003

ART DIRECTOR:
MARIO L'ÉCUYER
JEAN-LUC DENAT

DESIGNER:
MARIO L'ÉCUYER

PHOTOGRAPHER:
DWAYNE BROWN +
STOCK PHOTO

CLIENT:
CANADIAN
INSTITUTE OF
HEALTH RESEARCH

SOFTWARE AND
HARDWARE:
ILLUSTRATOR
PHOTOSHOP
QUARKXPRESS
MAC G4

MATERIALS:
MOHAWK
SUPERFINE +
GLAMA

PRINTING:
ST JOSEPH M.O.M.
PRINTING

109
IRIDIUM, A DESIGN AGENCY
CIHR/RX&D PROGRESS REPORT

CANADA

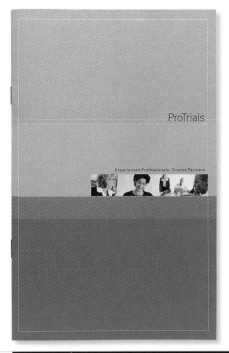

ProTrials

Experienced Professionals, Trusted Partners

USA

ART DIRECTOR:
LESLIE GUIDICE

DESIGNER:
STACY GUIDICE

CLIENT:
PROTRIALS
RESEARCH INC

SOFTWARE AND
HARDWARE:
ILLUSTRATOR
PHOTOSHOP
MAC G4

MATERIALS:
CURIOUS ICE BOLD
TEXT

PRINTING:
4/4

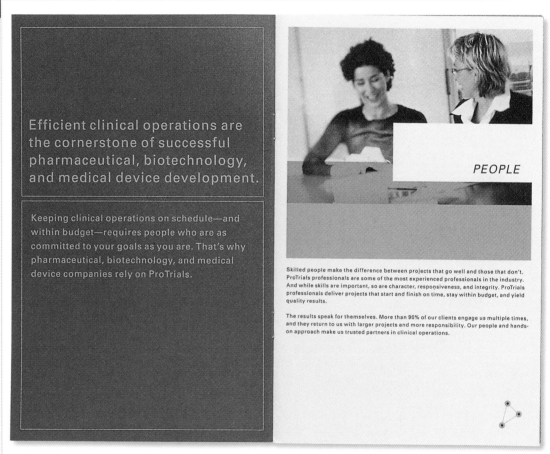

Efficient clinical operations are the cornerstone of successful pharmaceutical, biotechnology, and medical device development.

Keeping clinical operations on schedule—and within budget—requires people who are as committed to your goals as you are. That's why pharmaceutical, biotechnology, and medical device companies rely on ProTrials.

PEOPLE

Skilled people make the difference between projects that go well and those that don't. ProTrials professionals are some of the most experienced professionals in the industry. And while skills are important, so are character, responsiveness, and integrity. ProTrials professionals deliver projects that start and finish on time, stay within budget, and yield quality results.

The results speak for themselves. More than 90% of our clients engage us multiple times, and they return to us with larger projects and more responsibility. Our people and hands-on approach make us trusted partners in clinical operations.

COMMITMENT

110
ENERGY ENERGY DESIGN
PROTRIALS BROCHURE

TUSSEN DE BEDRIJVEN DOOR. EEN MOMENT VAN RUST. EVEN BIJPRATEN MET EEN GOEDE VRIEND. EEN WERELDLIJK RITUEEL.   ONDER HET GENOT VAN EEN GOED GLAS WIJN EN EEN FRISSE SALADE. DAARNA VERVOLGEN WE IEDER ONZE EIGEN WEG.

Busplatform

Indicatief programma

Op het Koningin Julianaplein bestaat het programma voor angeveer de helft uit wonen. Met name de hoger gelegen verdiepingen op deze locatie bieden unieke kansen voor wonen; de stad aan je voeten en uitzicht over Keekamp, Malieveld, Haagse Bos en de zee.

Ook op het Anna van Buerenplein en Babylon komen woningen die zowel mogelijk op het groengebied zijn georiënteerd.

Totaal programma

200.000 m2   120.000 m2   50.000 m2   30.000 m2
Kantoren   Woningen   Overig

Nieuwe parkeerplaatsen verdeeld naar functie

Kantoren   >   🚗🚗🚗🚗🚗🚗🚗🚗🚗🚗🚗🚗🚗 950 parkeerplaatsen
Woningen   >   🚗🚗🚗🚗🚗🚗🚗🚗 600 parkeerplaatsen
Winkels   >   🚗🚗🚗 200 parkeerplaatsen
Hotel/congres/overige > 🚗🚗🚗🚗🚗🚗🚗 500 parkeerplaatsen
Park & Ride   >   🚗🚗🚗 250 parkeerplaatsen

Totaal **2.500** parkeerplaatsen

111

2D3D
BROCHURE—DEN HAAG
NIEUW CENTRAAL

ART DIRECTORS:
GEA ZIEVERINK
YEW-KEE CHUNG
MICHAEL
BUCHENAUER

DESIGNERS:
GEA ZIEVERINK
YEW-KEE CHUNG
MICHAEL
BUCHENAUER

PHOTOGRAPHERS:
ERIC DE VRIES
PAUL LUNENBERG
PETER LEURINK
ARJAN BENNING
NEDERLANDSE
SPOORWEGEN
MULTI VASTGOED
GEMEENTE DEN
HAAG

CLIENT:
GEMEENTE DEN
HAAG

SOFTWARE AND
HARDWARE:
ILLUSTRATOR
PHOTOSHOP
QUARKXPRESS
MAC

MATERIALS:
GREY CARTON
2000GSM + OXFORD
160GSM

PRINTING:
OFFSET 4-PROCESS
COLORS

Anna van Buerenplein

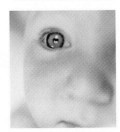

r:évolution

IRSC : VERS UN PROGRAMME
NATIONAL DE RECHERCHE EN SANTÉ

IRSC CIHR
Instituts de recherche   Canadian Institutes of
en santé du Canada   Health Research

Canada

112

IRIDIUM, A DESIGN AGENCY
R:EVOLUTION BROCHURE

CANADA

CREATIVE DIRECTOR
MARIO L'ÉCUYER

ART DIRECTOR:
JEAN-LUC DENAT

DESIGNER:
MARIO L'ÉCUYER

CLIENT:
CANADIAN
INSTITUTE OF
HEALTH RESEARCH

SOFTWARE AND
HARDWARE:
ILLUSTRATOR
PHOTOSHOP
QUARKXPRESS
MAC G4

MATERIALS:
POTLATCH
NORTHWEST
GLAMA

PRINTING:
ST. JOSEPH M.O.M.
PRINTING

USA

ASCENT

ART DIRECTOR:
YACHUN PENG

DESIGNERS:
YACHUN PENG
LEO RAYMUNDO

CLIENT:
SAFECO

SOFTWARE AND
HARDWARE:
FREEHAND
MAC G4

MATERIALS:
MOHAWK NAVAJO

PRINTING:
SAFECO PRINTING
PRESS

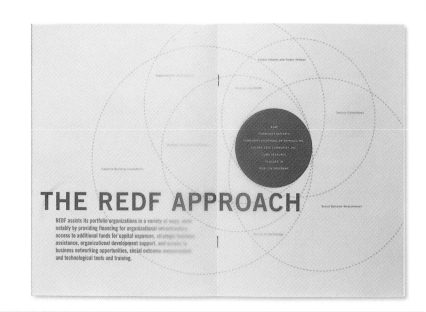

THE REDF APPROACH

REDF assists its portfolio organizations in a variety of ways, most notably by providing financing for organizational infrastructure, access to additional funds for capital expenses, strategic business assistance, organizational development support, and access to business networking opportunities, social outcome measurement, and technological tools and training.

114
CHEN DESIGN ASSOCIATES
REDF CORPORATE BROCHURE

USA

ART DIRECTOR:
JOSHUA C. CHEN

DESIGNERS:
MAX SPECTOR
LEON YU

PHOTOGRAPHER:
JENNY THOMAS

CLIENT:
ROBERTS
ENTERPRISE
DEVELOPMENT
FUND

SOFTWARE AND
HARDWARE:
ILLUSTRATOR
PHOTOSHOP
QUARKXPRESS
MAC

MATERIALS:
CENTURA DULL

PRINTING:
LITHOGRAPHIX

DESIGNER:
KAREN CHENG

CLIENT:
UNIVERSITY OF
WASHINGTON
SCHOOL OF ART

SOFTWARE:
ILLUSTRATOR
PHOTOSHOP
QUARKXPRESS

MATERIALS:
LUSTRO ARCHIVAL
DULL

PRINTING:
PROCESS COLOR +
AQUEOUS COATING

2000

F

(master of the fine arts)

M

A

university of washington
school of art

joline
ABBADESSA

thomas
ALBRECHT

roger
BOGERS

john
BYRD

maya
CHACHAVA

alan
CORKERY HAHN

mariko
DAIBO

wing
FONG

karen
GUTOWSKY

ayumi
HORIE

michelle
JACK

kamla
KAKARIA

james
LaCHANCE

robert
McCRORY

vaughn
RANDALL

phil
ROACH

lynn
SHEN

heather
SINCAVAGE

leslie
STRAKA

victoria
TCHETCHET

115
CHENG DESIGN
MASTER OF FINE ARTS EXHIBIT 2000

"Architecture . . . is the attempt to make what is originally a strange and alien environment more of our own, to transform space into place, so that instead of being cast into a strange and alien world we are allowed to dwell."

Karsten Harries

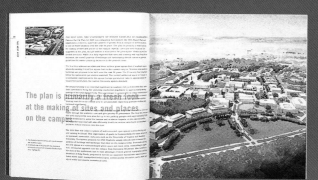

The plan is primarily a fresh look at the making of sites and places on the campus

116
POULIN + MORRIS
UNC AT CHARLOTTE CAMPUS
MASTER PLAN

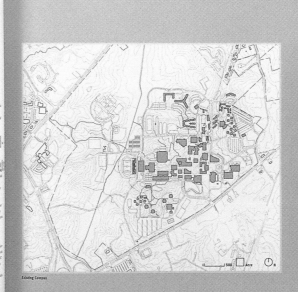

Existing Campus

3.0

ANALYSIS

USA

Phase Two: Years 6 - 10

5.0

ART DIRECTOR:
L RICHARD POULIN

DESIGNER:
BRIAN BRINDISI

CLIENT:
COOPER,
ROBERTSON &
PARTNERS

SOFTWARE:
QUARKXPRESS

MATERIALS:
MOHAWK 50/10
PLUS

PRINTING:
QUALITY PRINTING

AUTHORED BY
Fay Twersky

BTW Consultants - influencing change

WITH INPUT AND CONTRIBUTIONS FROM
Rick Aubry, Rubicon Programs

Tina Dauser, CompuMentor

Jane Fischberg, Rubicon Programs

Danny Feng, Dayspring Technologies

Laura Lanzerotti, BTW Consultants

Wes Reed, Third Sector

Melinde Tison, The Roberts Enterprise Development Fund

An Information OASIS:
The Design and Implementation of
Comprehensive and Customized Client
Information and Tracking Systems

OASIS is a planning process and project that has been
generously supported by The Roberts Enterprise
Development Fund, the Charles and Helen Schwab
Foundation, The William and Flora Hewlett Foundation,
the Sandra Foundation, the Flaherty Foundation,
and the Peavey Family Fund.

This publication is made possible by a generous
contribution from The William and Flora Hewlett
Foundation.

117

CHEN DESIGN ASSOCIATES
AN INFORMATION OASIS

USA

ART DIRECTOR:	DESIGNERS:	PHOTOGRAPHER:	CLIENT:	SOFTWARE AND HARDWARE:	MATERIALS:	PRINTING:
JOSHUA C. CHEN	MAX SPECTOR	JENNY THOMAS	ROBERTS	ILLUSTRATOR	STORA ENSO	LITHOGRAPHIX
	JOSHUA C. CHEN		ENTERPRISE	PHOTOSHOP	CENTURA DULL	
			DEVELOPMENT	QUARKXPRESS	100# T, 100# C.	
			FUND	MAC	GLAMA NATURAL	
					21.25# T CLEAR	

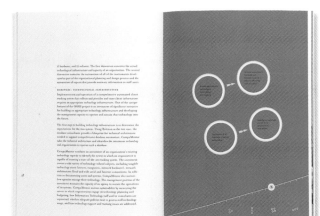

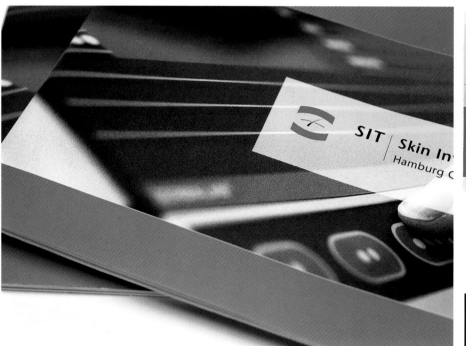

118
MARIUS FAHRNER DESIGN
SIT

ART DIRECTOR:
MARIUS FAHRNER

DESIGNER:
MARIUS FAHRNER

CLIENT:
SIT

SOFTWARE:
FREEHAND

PRINTING:
2-COLOR OFFSET

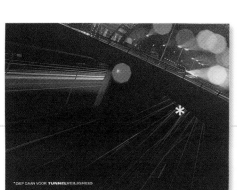

*DIEP GAAN VOOR **TUNNELVEILIGHEID**

BRENG HET BELANG VAN VEILIGHEID AAN HET LICHT

OPEN

VEILIGHEID IS EEN ESSENTIEEL ELEMENT DAT VANAF HET BEGIN THUISHOORT IN HET ONTWIKKELINGSPROCES VAN TUNNELS. NIET IN HET MINST VANWEGE HAAR HOGE KOSTEN. HET KOSTENBATEN PERSPECTIEF VOORAF IN DE

BESLUITVORMING BETREKKEN, VOORKOMT DAT HET PRIJSKAARTJE VOOR TUNNELVEILIGHEID PAS 'NÁ DE KOOP' WORDT OPGESPELD.

ART DIRECTOR: YEW-KEE CHUNG	DESIGNER: YEW-KEE CHUNG	PHOTOGRAPHER: ERIC DE VRIES	CLIENT: PROJECTGROEP TUNNELVEILIGHEID	SOFTWARE AND HARDWARE: PHOTOSHOP QUARKXPRESS MAC	MATERIALS: COVER: CURIOUS METALLICS 300GSM INSIDE: MUNKEN LYNX 150GSM	PRINTING: 4-COLOR OFFSET

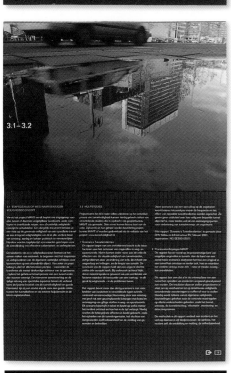

3.1–3.2

THE NETHERLANDS

2 –2.1

2 TUNNELVEILIGHEID IN NEDERLAND

In een tunnel loopt men andere risico's dan in de open ruimte. Alhoewel de kans klein is kunnen incidenten of ongevallen in de besloten ruimte van een tunnel in korte tijd ernstige gevolgen hebben. Met name brand, ontsnapping van rook en van giftige of explosieve stoffen zijn gevaren die in enkele minuten tijd kans lopen om uit te groeien tot levensgevaarlijke rampen met dreiging van veel slachtoffers. Voor mensen die moeten vluchten is het in een tunnel nu eenmaal lastiger om een goed heenkomen te zoeken dan in de open ruimte. En voor hulpdiensten zijn de kansen om er snel en effectief levensreddend op te treden beduidend minder, zoals de laatste jaren maar al te zeer bleek bij calamiteiten in Alpentunnels (Gotthard, Mont Blanc, Tauern, Kaprun).

Gezien de ernst van deze risico's heeft tunnelveiligheid in Nederland de laatste twintig jaar zonder twijfel de aandacht gekregen die ze verdient. Ook in Nederland droeg een tunnelbrand daaraan het nodige bij. Deze calamiteit in de Velsertunnel (1978, 4 doden) leidde enkele jaren later tot nieuwe richtlijnen voor de uitrusting van wegtunnels. Mede hierdoor hebben de meeste daarvan in ons land thans gescheiden buizen voor beide rijrichtingen, zijn ze goed verlicht en worden ze zeer degelijk onderhouden. Verder is er vrijwel altijd een ventilatiesysteem dat rook en dampen kan wegblazen en beschikken grote tunnels – ook die van spoor en metro – doorgaans over beheerders die getraind zijn om adequaat om te gaan met incidenten.

De richtlijnen, in 1991 vastgesteld door de Werkgroep Uitrusting Tunnels (WUT) worden door opdrachtgevers, ontwerpers en beheerders gebruikt om een basisniveau van tunnelveiligheid te realiseren. Tien jaar geleden waren ze een duidelijke uitbreiding, tegenwoordig zijn ze veeleer synoniem met een standaardbenadering.

De groei van het aantal tunnels en hun grotere diversiteit vereisen derhalve een nieuwe fase in het veiligheidsbeleid voor tunnels; een fase niet enkel met nieuwe en aangescherpte richtlijnen maar ook met een andere benaderingswijze. De Tweede Kamer en maatschappelijke organisaties dringen hierop aan, maar – niet in de laatste plaats – ook ontwerpers vragen erom.

2.1 TUNNELVEILIGHEID. WIE IS VERANTWOORDELIJK?

Het plan om een tunnel aan te leggen kan afkomstig zijn van allerlei verschillende partijen. Naast gemeenten en provincies zijn tegenwoordig steeds vaker publiekprivate organisaties en particuliere ondernemingen initiatiefnemer op dit gebied. De motieven tot tunnelaanleg zijn velerlei. Ze variëren van een verbeterde regionale ontsluiting (Westerscheldetunnel) en de bescherming van milieu en landschap (HSL-tunnel door het Groene Hart) tot meervoudig ruimtegebruik in stedelijke gebieden (Overkluizing Zuid-as Amsterdam). Momenteel zijn diverse nieuwe en grote tunnels in aanbouw. Plannen voor tientallen grote tunnels en overkappingen staan op stapel. De verantwoordelijkheid voor de veiligheid van die tunnels wordt gedeeld. Het rijk stelt de algemene wettelijke eisen aan de veiligheid van bouwwerken en aan de uitrusting van tunnels in het bijzonder. Gemeenten moeten toezien op de navolging daarvan door het beoordelen en afgeven van bouwvergunningen. Daarnaast behoort de rampenbestrijding tot hun wettelijke taak. Lokale overheden moeten kiezen voor welke risicovolle objecten, waaronder tunnels, een rampbestrijdingsplan geboden is. De eerste en directe verantwoordelijkheid voor veiligheid in tunnels ligt echter bij de eigenaren en beheerders van bouwwerk. Zij moeten zorgen dat zo'n bouwwerk veilig is en blijft.

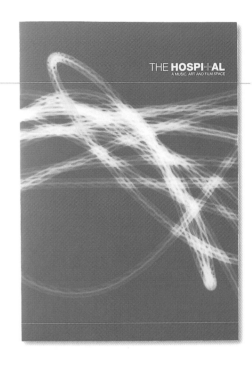

ART DIRECTORS:
PAUL WEST
PAULA BENSON

DESIGNERS:
PAUL WEST
PAULA BENSON

CLIENT:
THE HOSPITAL

SOFTWARE:
FREEHAND
PHOTOSHOP

MATERIALS:
CONSORT ROYAL

PRINTING:
LITHO

120
FORM
HOSPITAL BROCHURE

Who are we?
The Hospital Group is owned by Paul G. Allen, who co-founded Microsoft, and run in collaboration with Dave Stewart, film maker, musician and Covent Garden resident.

In the USA, Paul G. Allen is currently developing **Experience Music Project** in Seattle, a 140,000 square foot interactive music museum, opening in 2000, providing 100 jobs and extensive education programmes.

We have been running education programmes in Seattle since 1995, as we work with local partners to take education into the community even before our building is ready. We have run workshops on the music business, video and film production, developed music curriculum materials for 10-18 year olds and even run music workshops for toddlers.

We also have **Experience Arts Camp** for 8-14 year olds, giving local children training in music, film, the visual arts, drama and creative technologies. We arranged for 30% of the places to be funded by sponsorship for those who couldn't afford the cost.

Paul G. Allen also has a wide range of commercial interests in many new media and technology ventures and other fields related to the proposed Hospital development. We have an independent film company which has made **Inspirations**, a documentary directed by Michael Apted featuring musician David Bowie, painter Roy Lichtenstein, glass artist Dale Chihuly, architect Tadao Ando, dancer Louise Lecavalier, choreographer Edouard Lock and sculptor Nora Naranjo-Morse. **Inspirations II** is now in production, focusing on the creative process in science.

We are also filming **Titus** with Julie Taymor directing a version of Titus Andronicus, starring Sir Anthony Hopkins, Jessica Lange and Alan Cumming, with a behind the camera team including four Oscar® nominees.

Our wealth of experience and contacts in the international arts, entertainment and business communities will help ensure the success of The Hospital.

Timetable.

1992	St Paul's Hospital closure.
1996	Building purchased by The Hospital Group.
1997	Cleaning up process begins.
1998	First planning application refused. Revised application to be submitted.
1999	Revised application submitted.
	· Visitor centre opens at 41 Endell Street.
	· Educational pilot programmes planned.
	· Housing gain for Camden.*

Additional off-site educational initiatives.*

2001 The Hospital will be open and operational after an 18 month building and fitting out schedule.*

*Subject to planning approval.

...tional multi-arts facility for music, film and art, built on the ...dict St Paul's Hospital site in Covent Garden. ...facility will provide unprecedented opportunities for collaboration between world-renowned artists.

THE HOSPITAL
A MUSIC, ART AND FILM SPACE

UK

ART DIRECTORS:
CHIARA GRANDESSO
LIONELLO BOREAN

DESIGNERS:
CHIARA GRANDESSO
LIONELLO BOREAN

CLIENT:
CHIARA GRANDESSO
LIONELLO BOREAN

MATERIALS:
ENVELOPE WITH
EMBOSSED PRINT

PRINTING:
CMYK + GOLD INK
+ 1 PANTONE

121
USINE DE BOUTONS
MAYAPLUM BIRTH
ANNOUCEMENT

ITALY

HITEC-LOTEC IS A THREE YEAR LOTTERY-FUNDED PROJECT WHICH EXPLORES THE RELATIONSHIP BETWEEN CRAFT AND INDUSTRY THROUGH THE USE OF NEW TECHNOLOGY AND MATERIALS.

122

THIRTEEN DESIGN
HITEC-LOTEC CATALOG

ART DIRECTOR:
DANNY JENKINS

DESIGNERS:
DANNY JENKINS
RYAN WILLS

PHOTOGRAPHERS:
MARCUS GINNS
GRANTLY LYNCH
DANNY JENKINS

CLIENT:
THE CRAFT
CONSORTIUM
FOR NOW AND THE
CRAFTS COUNCIL

SOFTWARE:
ILLUSTRATOR
PHOTOSHOP
QUARKXPRESS

PAPER/MATERIAL:
ORCHARD
SUPERFINE +
FORMATION
SUPERFINE

PRINTING:
4-COLOR PROCESS
+ SEAL

UK

123
BOSTOCK & POLLITT
REGENERATION SCHEME PROMO

ART DIRECTOR:
PAT GLOVER

DESIGNER:
PAT GLOVER

CLIENT:
LEND LEASE

UK

ravensbourne
college of
design and communication
www.ravensbourne.ac.uk

Ravensbourne is a University Sector College with a
distinctive personality and creative tradition, focalised on
a single site campus within easy reach of central London.
Our mission is to creatively apply digital technology
to design and communication.

2002/03

ra
ens
u
e.

v
bo
rn

®

ravensbourne
college of
design and communicatior
www.ravensbourne.ac.uk

Ravensbourne is a University Sector College with a
distinctive personality and creative tradition, focalised on
a single site campus within easy reach of central London.
Our mission is to creatively apply digital technology
to design and communication

2002/03

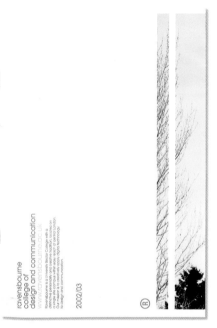

ravensbourne
college of
design and communication
www.ravensbourne.ac.uk

Ravensbourne is a University Sector College with a
distinctive personality and creative tradition, focalised on
a single site campus within easy reach of central London.
Our mission is to creatively apply digital technology
to design and communication.

2002/03

®

ART DIRECTORS:
BEN PARKER
PAUL AUSTIN

DESIGNERS:
BEN PARKER
PAUL AUSTIN

PHOTOGRAPHER:
LEE MAWDSLEY

CLIENT:
RAVENSBOURNE
COLLEGE OF
DESIGN AND
COMMUNICATION

PRINTING:
PERIVAN

ravensbourne
college of
design and
communication
2002/03
www.
raven

SELF-PROMOTIONAL BROCHURES

STILRADAR // CHEN DESIGN ASSOCIATES // SAS // FROST DESIGN // IRIDIUM, A DESIGN AGENCY
IRON DESIGN // FORM // ELFEN // GRAPHICULTURE // BISQIT DESIGN // FORMAT DESIGN //
WILLOUGHBY DESIGN GROUP // LEAD DOG DIGITAL // KOLEGRAMDESIGN // KO CRÉATION //
USINE DE BOUTONS // LOEWY GROUP // HADE MADE GROUP // THIRTEEN DESIGN //

.05

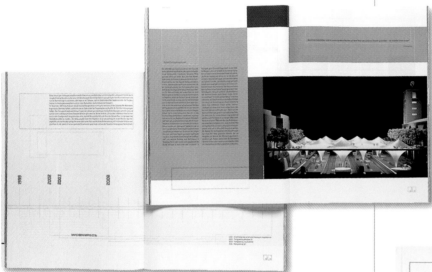

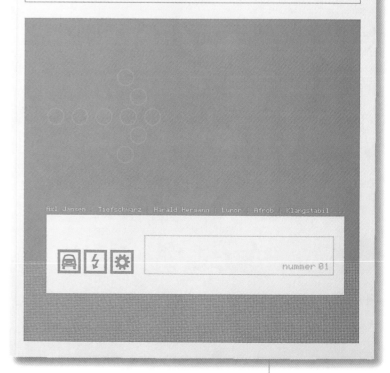

ART DIRECTORS:
RAPHAEL POHLAND
SIMONE WINTER

CLIENT:
SELF-PROMOTION
(DIPLOMA)

SOFTWARE:
FREEHAND
PHOTOSHOP
QUARKXPRESS

MATERIALS:
ZANDERS IKONO
SILK

PRINTING:
OFFSET

USABLE - DO NOT DIS

WEBAPPFACTORY CORPORATE IDENTITY SYSTEM

USA

ART DIRECTOR:	DESIGNERS:	PHOTOGRAPHERS:	CLIENT:	SOFTWARE AND HARDWARE:	MATERIALS:	PRINTING:
JOSHUA C. CHEN	LEON YU MAX SPECTOR JUSTIN COYNE JOSHUA C. CHEN	MAX SPECTOR LEON YU JUSTIN COYNE	CHEN DESIGN ASSOCIATES	ILLUSTRATOR PHOTOSHOP QUARKXPRESS MAC	HAMMERMILL REGALIA ULTRA WHITE 80C	MADISON STREET PRESS

NO VACANCY

Over the past decade, the cost of rental housing has risen faster than inflation and faster than the incomes of the average California family. Rental housing costs increased 38 percent in San Francisco...

Only 12 percent of households can afford a median price home...

20% of San Franciscans spend over 60% of their income on rent

TEMPORARY SHELTER FACILITIES MEET THE NEEDS OF ONLY ONE IN SIX HOMELESS INDIVIDUALS AND ONE IN FIVE HOMELESS FAMILIES

SAN FRANCISCO'S VACANCY RATE: < 1%

All statistics and quotations from the San Francisco Tenants Union

ART DIRECTOR:
GILMAR WENDT

DESIGNER:
GILMAR WENDT

CLIENT:
SAS

SOFTWARE:
INDESIGN

MATERIALS:
PHOENIXMOTION
XENON

PRINTING:
ROSBEEK

UK

127

SAS
CMYKRGB—INSIDE SAS

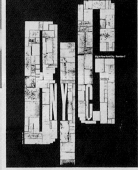

sweet

ART DIRECTORS:
VINCE FROST
BALWANT AHIRA

DESIGNERS:
VINCE FROST
BALWANT AHIRA

CLIENT:
FROST DESIGN

MATERIALS:
REDEEM 115GSM BY
FENNER PAPER

PRINTING:
PRINCIPAL COLOR
(LITHO)

UK

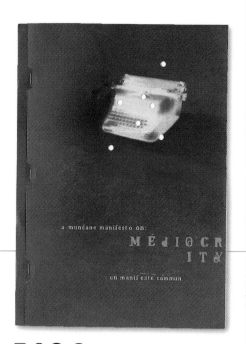

129

IRIDIUM, A DESIGN AGENCY
A MUNDANE MANIFESTO ON MEDIOCRITY

ART DIRECTORS:
JEAN-LUC DENAT
MARIO L'ÉCUYER

DESIGNER:
MARIO L'ÉCUYER

PHOTOGRAPHER:
HEADLIGHT
INNOVATIVE IMAGERY

CLIENT:
ROLLAND INC

SOFTWARE AND
HARDWARE:
ILLUSTRATOR
PHOTOSHOP
QUARKXPRESS
MAC G4

MATERIALS:
ROLLAND MOTIF

PRINTING:
LOMOR PRINTERS

CANADA

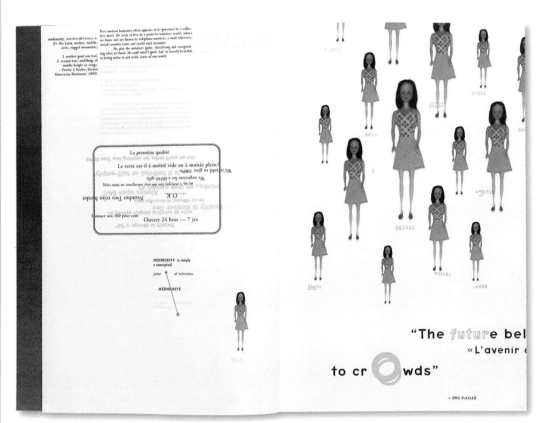

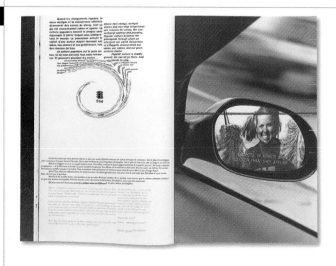

130
IRON DESIGN
IRON DESIGN BROCHURE

ART DIRECTOR:	DESIGNERS:	CLIENT:	SOFTWARE:	MATERIALS:	PRINTING:
TODD EDMUNDS	TODD EDMUNDS	IRON DESIGN	ILLUSTRATOR	100LB DULL-COATED	CURCIO PRINTING +
	TANA EBAUGH		PHOTOSHOP	COVER	JOHNSON CITY PRESS
			QUARKXPRESS		

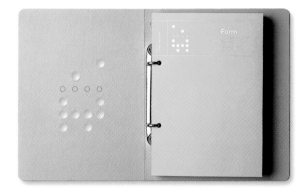

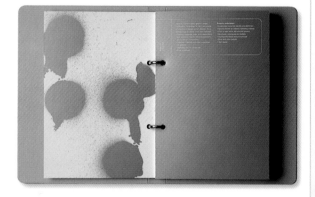

UK

ART DIRECTORS:
PAULA BENSON
PAUL WEST

DESIGNERS:
PAULA BENSON
PAUL WEST

CLIENT:
FORM

SOFTWARE:
FREEHAND

MATERIALS:
CONSORT ROYAL
SILK +
POLYPROPELENE

PRINTING:
LITHO INSERTS +
SCREEN-PRINTED
COVER

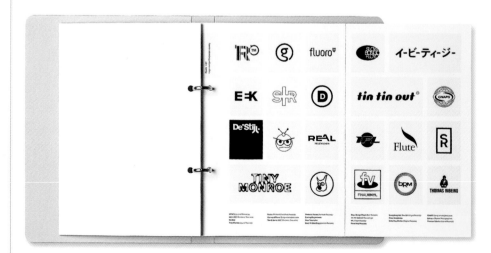

www.elfen.co.uk

ART DIRECTOR:
COMBINED

DESIGNERS:
GUTO EVANS
GWION PRYDDERCH
MATHEW JAMES

CLIENT:
ELFEN

SOFTWARE:
FREEHAND
PHOTOSHOP
QUARKXPRESS

MATERIALS:
CYCLUS OFFSET

PRINTING:
LITHO

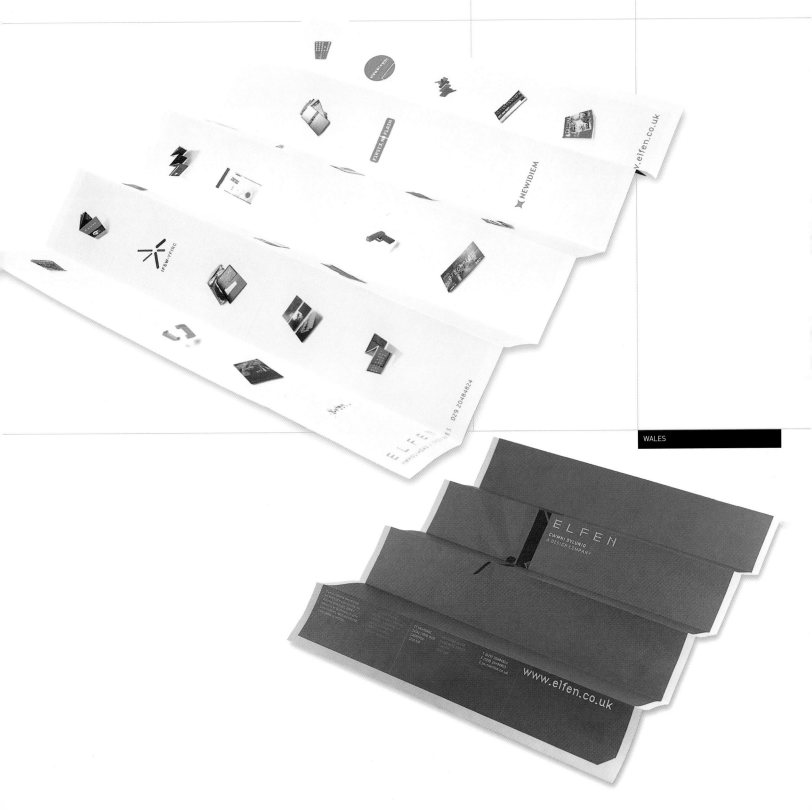

WALES

Beaten by Neo Nazis. January in Minneapolis. Stripped naked. Thrown from bridge. I am dead. Much later. Found. Toe tagged. Placed in morgue. Wake. See tag. Scream. I am alive.

Michael Walter Johnson

The end.

USA

I GET UP AT 5 IN THE MORNING AND I DON'T HATE IT. Twelve Chevy Suburbans and twenty five years later, Steve still digs his job. Exclusive to one company, an engineering firm with clients spread across the map. He's seen many jobs inside and outside of his company, proclaiming his the best of all. Every day is different, every day is still worthy of that 5 a.m. wake-up call.

BIG HIT AND RUN. He gets the best of people. All the personal interaction he needs. Just enough, not too much. Swing in for an anniversary party, a birthday party, have a slice of cake, pizza, a handful of mixed nuts and move on.

GREEN THUMBS ON THE WHEEL. A double lot in south Minneapolis and a family history in horticulture makes Steve a favorite with the ladies. Just watch 'em beam as he slides in with a gathering of fresh flowers hand-selected from the Bachleitner Gardens.

ANTIQUE ROAD SHOWMAN. The secret life of Steve Bachleitner—arranging and running appraisal and estate sales. Digging the remains and remnants of an existence. In dim attics and hat boxes and stubborn drawers are the letters, photographs and props of lives lived and lost. A skill possibly inherited from his father, the candy, cigarette and gum salesman, who would drag his boys to the dump and drag home assorted unmemorable finds. A collector in his own right, he warns us all to watch for the sale notice on the Steve Bachleitner estate—he guarantees it'll be a good one. (Not too soon Steve, we can wait.)

Steve Bachleitner
window on the world

I'M A HAPPY GUY
He's a happy guy.

133
GRAPHICULTURE
"DIRECT"—THE COURIER BOOK

DESIGNER:
BETH MUELLER

CLIENT:
GRAPHICULTURE

MATERIALS:
WAUSAU PAPERS

PRINTING:
LANDMARK COLOUR
COMMUNICATIONS

Bob Alexander
noteworthy

" Bisqit is a team with attitude and a flexible approach, that always meets deadlines. I had a lot of fun working with Bisqit and I'd certainly recommend them."

Elaine Devereaux, Public Relations Department, T-Motion

Focusing on the key message 'get out more', T-Motion wanted to promote its internet services for mobiles with a series of communication materials that targeted the savvy mobile consumer. Using witty photography and bold type, this campaign served to position T-Motion as the new mobile on-line service with attitude.

BISQIT

UNext is the independent market leader in the delivery of executive learning, via the Internet.

This direct mail piece, with its powerful call to action, was designed to engage their target market and provoke a response.

UK

DESIGNER:	CLIENT:	SOFTWARE AND	PRINTING:
DAPHNE DIAMANT	BISQIT DESIGN	HARDWARE:	THE OAK TREE
		ILLUSTRATOR	PRESS
		PHOTOSHOP	
		QUARKXPRESS	
		MAC	

FORMAT DESIGN

GERMANY

135
FORMAT DESIGN
FORMAT DESIGN PORTFOLIO

DESIGNER:	ILLUSTRATOR:	CLIENT:	SOFTWARE AND	MATERIALS:	PRINTING:
KNUT ETTLING	KNUT ETTLING	FORMAT DESIGN	HARDWARE:	300G PHOENIX	4-COLORS
			FREEHAND	MOTION	
			MAC		

WHAT ARE OUR GUIDING PRINCIPLES?
WHAT WILL NEVER CHANGE...

WHAT IS OUR REASON FOR COMING TO WORK EACH DAY?
WHAT IS THE SOUL OF OUR COMPANY?

our vision is...

WILLOUGHBY DESIGN GROUP

DEFINE

FUTURE PLANNING RETREAT 2002

ART DIRECTOR:
ANN WILLOUGHBY

DESIGNER:
TRENTON KENAGY

CLIENT:
WILLOUGHBY
DESIGN GROUP

SOFTWARE AND
HARDWARE:
QUARKXPRESS
MAC

MATERIALS:
OFFSET

PRINTING:
IN-HOUSE

?

we have a great reputation, clients, people and work, so why?

WILLOUGHBY DESIGN GROUP

DO WE HAVE TO CHANGE?

in order to prosper tomorrow

FUTURE PLANNING RETREAT 2002

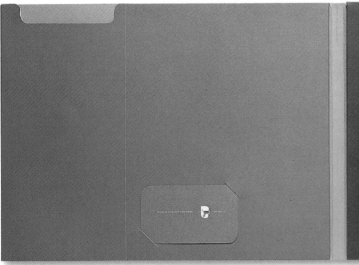

ART DIRECTOR:
NATALIE LAM

DESIGNER:
NATALIE LAM

CLIENT:
LEAD DOG DIGITAL

SOFTWARE:
ILLUSTRATOR
QUARKXPRESS

MATERIALS:
FRENCH

PRINTING:
SEIDEL

137

LEAD DOG DIGITAL
LEAD DOG DIGITAL BROCHURE

qué   cho   ema   res

ART DIRECTOR:
MIKE TEIXEIRA

DESIGNER:
MIKE TEIXEIRA

CLIENT:
KOLÉGRAMDESIGN

SOFTWARE AND
HARDWARE:
QUARKXPRESS
MAC

PRINTING:
DU PROGRÈS
ALBION
LOMOR PRINTING

CANADA

ART DIRECTORS:
POL BARIL
DENIS DULUDE
ANNIE LACHAPELLE

DESIGNERS:
POL BARIL
DENIS DULUDE
ANNIE LACHAPELLE

CLIENT:
KO CREATION

SOFTWARE AND
HARDWARE:
ILLUSTRATOR
PHOTOSHOP
QUARKXPRESS
MAC G3
MAC G4

MATERIALS:
INSIDE: SAPPI
STROBE SILK 100LB
COVER: KRAFT
CARDBOARD

PRINTING:
HEIDELBERG
SPEEDMASTER 102
SHEETFED PRESS.
LINE SCREEN: 175
LPI; 4-COLORS
PROCESS + SATIN
WATER-BASED
VARNISH, 28 X 40,
5-COLORS + WATER-
BASED UNIT

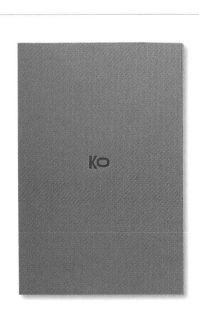

139
KO CRÉATION
SCRAPBOOK 03

ART DIRECTORS: DESIGNERS: CLIENT: PRINTING:
LIONELLO BOREAN   LIONELLO BOREAN   NARDUZZI   CMYK + SILVER
CHIRARA GRANDESSO   CHIRARA GRANDESSO   PHOTOGRAPHER

ITALY

140
USINE DE BOUTONS
NARDUZZI SELF-PROMOTION

ART DIRECTOR:
CLARE WILSON

DESIGNER:
VICKY TRAINER

PHOTOGRAPHER:
PHIL SAYER

MATERIALS:
ROBERT HORNE

PRINTING:
PERIVAN GROUP LTD

141

LOEWY GROUP
LOEWY BROCHURE

What's going on out there? The year is 2010. Your rival's brand is dead. Why?

ART DIRECTOR:	DESIGNERS:	CLIENT:	SOFTWARE AND	MATERIALS:	PRINTING:
ALESSANDRO ESTERI	DAVIDE PREMUMI	HAND MADE GROUP	HARDWARE:	FEDRIGONI SYMBOL	OFFSET +
	ALESSANDRO ESTERI		QUARKXPRESS	PEARL	SILKSCREEN
			MAC		

142
HADE MADE GROUP
SELF-PROMO PROFILE

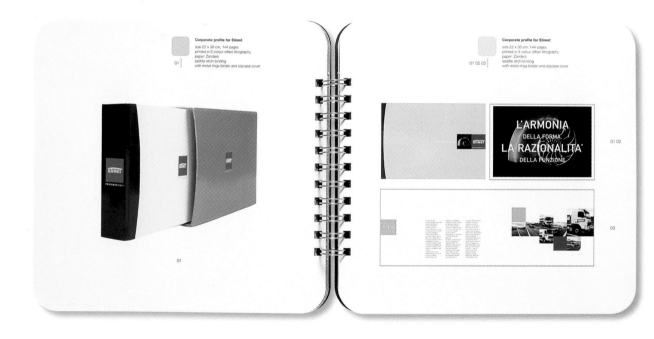

Corporate profile for Stimet
size 22 x 30 cm, 144 pages
printed in 5 colour offset lithography
paper: Zanders
saddle stich binding
with metal rings binder and slipcase cover

01

Corporate profile for Stimet
size 22 x 30 cm, 144 pages
printed in 5 colour offset lithography
paper: Zanders
saddle stich binding
with metal rings binder and slipcase cover

01 02 03

L'ARMONIA
DELLA FORMA
LA RAZIONALITA'
DELLA FUNZIONE

ITALY

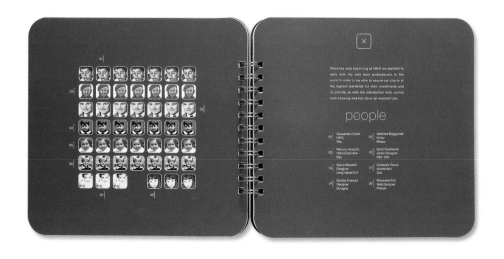

Since the very beginning at HMG we decided to work with the very best professionals in the world in order to be able to assure our clients of the highest standards for their investments and to provide us with the satisfaction which comes from knowing one has done an excellent job.

people

ART DIRECTORS:
JOHN UNDERWOOD
DANNY JENKINS
NICK HAND

DESIGNER:
JOHN UNDERWOOD

PHOTOGRAPHERS:
PETER THORPE
MARCUS GINNS

CLIENT:
THIRTEEN DESIGN

SOFTWARE:
ILLUSTRATOR
PHOTOSHOP
QUARKXPRESS

MATERIALS:
ESSENTIAL GLOSS
DUTCHMAN

PRINTING:
4-COLOR PROCESS +
2 SPECIAL PMS
COLORS + SEALANT

UK

143
THIRTEEN DESIGN
THIRTEEN WORK BOOKS

ARTS, ENTERTAINMENT
AND EVENTS BROCHURES

FROST DESIGN // MARCO MOROSINI // BISQIT DESIGN // REBECCA FOSTER DESIGN // SAS //
FAUXPAS // POULIN + MORRIS // BLUE RIVER DESIGN // HAT-TRICK DESIGN // CHRISTINE FENT +
GILMAR WENDT // HAMBLY & WOOLLEY // NEW MOMENT // KO CRÉATION // KOLÉGRAMDESIGN //
NET INTEGRATORS – NET DESIGN // STEERS MCGILLAN // FABIO ONGARATO DESIGN //
NB:STUDIO // SAGMEISTER INC // CHIMERA DESIGN // CARTER WONG TOMLIN // FORM5 + BÜRO7 /
USINE DE BOUTONS // PING-PONG DESIGN // HATCH CREATIVE // SAYLES GRAPHIC DESIGN

:06

UK

ART DIRECTOR:
VINCE FROST

DESIGNERS:
VINCE FROST
SONYA DYAKOVA

CLIENT:
THE WAPPING
PROJECT

MATERIALS:
CHROMALUX 700
90GSM (BROAD-
SHEET)

PRINTING:
PRINCIPAL COLOR
(LITHO)

144
FROST DESIGN
THE WAPPING PROJECT NYC

UNA, CENTO, MILLE PELOTA.
THE PELOTA AND ITS MANY FACETS.

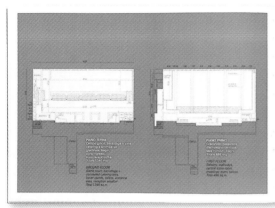

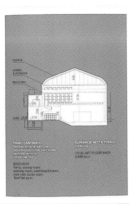

145

MARCO MOROSINI
PELOTA

ITALY

ART DIRECTOR:
MARCO MOROSINI

DESIGNER:
MARCO MOROSINI

ILLUSTRATOR:
MARCO MOROSINI

CLIENT:
PELOTA SRL

SOFTWARE AND
HARDWARE:
QUARKXPRESS
MAC

MATERIALS:
COATED 300 PR
PAPER

PRINTING:
REMOGRAFICA
BOLOGNA

DESIGNER:
DAPHNE DIAMANT
PATRICK DEVLIN

PHOTOGRAPHER:
RANKIN

CLIENT:
WORLD SNOOKER

SOFTWARE AND
HARDWARE:
ILLUSTRATOR
PHOTOSHOP
QUARKXPRESS
MAC

MATERIALS:
MEDLEY AND PVC
PACK

PRINTING:
MIDAS

UK

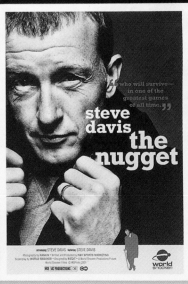

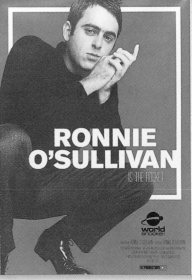

ReDesign
Sustainability in New British Design

UK

Greater London Authority Headquarters

Architect: Foster & Partners

Why do animals curl up into a ball to keep warm? To reduce the surface area from which they can lose heat. The future home for London's new strategic administration follows the same principle, in stunning style. Visually open and transparent, its form is derived from a sphere, which has 25% less surface area than a cube of the same volume. Aligned to minimise direct sunlight from the south, and drawing up ground water from two deep boreholes to cool the air, the building is expected to consume just one quarter of the energy required by an equivalent, typical - straight-edged - office building.

www.london.gov.uk/gla/
www.fosterandpartners.com

More than hot air: combination of natural shading and ventilation, and recycling of heat from computers, lights and people, mean the GLA building requires no boilers or chillers »

23

147
REBECCA FOSTER DESIGN
REDESIGN: SUSTAINABILITY IN
NEW BRITISH DESIGN

ART DIRECTOR:
REBECCA FOSTER

PHOTOGRAPHER:
REBECCA FOSTER

CLIENT:
BRITISH COUNCIL

SOFTWARE AND
HARDWARE:
ILLUSTRATOR
PHOTOSHOP
QUARKXPRESS
MAC G4

MATERIALS:
CHALLENGER
VELVET 400GSM +
170GSM

PRINTING:
4-COLOR + PMS 804C
(FLUORESCENT) +
SEAL

Supermarked på lavenergi
Sainsbury's

Supermarkedenes popularitet i Storbritannia skyldes hverken arkitektur eller energieffektivitet, men ren bekvemmelighet. Dette kan endre seg med Sainsbury's nye supermarked i Greenwich, som gjennom flott design og en mengde energibesparende tiltak har blitt et virkelig trivelig sted å handle dagligvarer. Butikken har sørgeshorter som et "sagiasmet" glasstak som slipper inn naturlig lys via datastyrte sjalusier, passiv "hakilufts"-ventilasjon, jordvoller rundt butikken som isolasjon, oppvarming fra en kombinert varme- og kraftstasjon i selve bygningen, og et kjølesystem som sirkulerer borehullsvann i gulvet. Lavere utgifter til strøm og brensel – og mer fornøyde kunder – har ført til at butikkjeden vil vurdere å gå løs for flere av disse lavenergi-satsingene i alle nye butikkprosjekter.

www.chetwood-associates.com

Sainsbury's supermarked i Greenwich er det første i verden som har blitt designet ut fra grunnleggende prinsipper, med miljøhensyn øverst på listen »

10

INDICATION
VORZEICHEN
VOORTEKEN

UWE POTH

THE OFFICE
ORCHESTRA

ANDREA CHAPPELL AND CHERRY GODDARD

PARADISE
IS ALWAYS
WHERE
YOU'VE BEEN

SANDY SYKES

148

SAS
INSIDE COVER
EXHIBITION CATALOG

A TO Z

ABRAHAMS

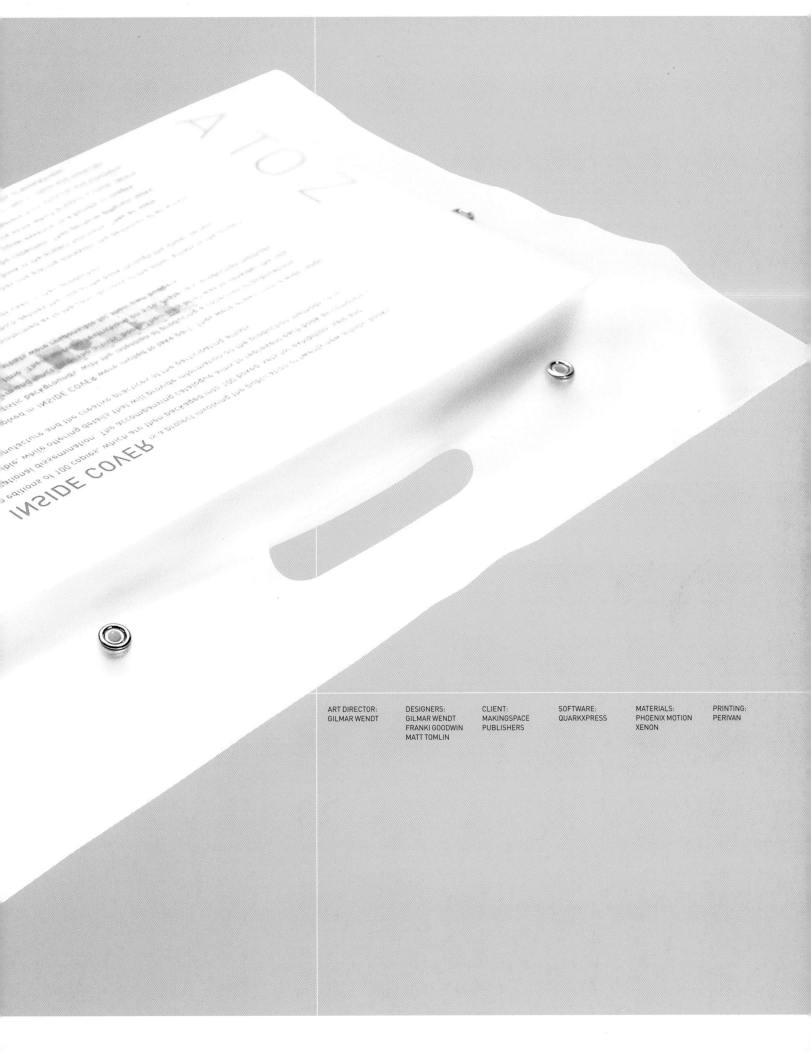

ART DIRECTOR:
GILMAR WENDT

DESIGNERS:
GILMAR WENDT
FRANKI GOODWIN
MATT TOMLIN

CLIENT:
MAKINGSPACE
PUBLISHERS

SOFTWARE:
QUARKXPRESS

MATERIALS:
PHOENIX MOTION
XENON

PRINTING:
PERIVAN

SWITZERLAND

ART DIRECTOR:	DESIGNER:	CLIENT:	SOFTWARE AND HARDWARE:	MATERIALS:	PRINTING:
MARTIN STILLHART	MARTIN STILLHART	SWISS NATIONAL TRUST	QUARKXPRESS MAC	Z-OFFSET W	OFFSET

society for environmental graphic design
1999 design awards

society for environmental graphic design
1999 design awards

150
POULIN + MORRIS
SEGD

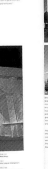

society for environmental graphic design
1999 design awards

DESIGNERS:	CLIENT:	SOFTWARE:	MATERIALS:	PRINTING:
L. RICHARD POULIN	SOCIETY FOR	QUARKXPRESS	SAPPI LUSTRO	QUALITY PRINTING
DOUGLAS MORRIS	ENVIRONMENTAL			
	GRAPHIC DESIGN			

ART DIRECTOR:
REBECCA FOSTER

ILLUSTRATOR:
REBECCA FOSTER

CLIENT:
PIAGGIO/ACTION ON
ADDICTION

SOFTWARE AND
HARDWARE:
ILLUSTRATOR
QUARKXPRESS
MAC G4

MATERIALS:
COVER: CYCLUS
PRINT 115 GSM
TEXT: CHALLENGER
VELVET 170 GSM

PRINTING:
COVER: DOUBLE HIT
PMS & M/C MATTE
SEALER
TEXT: 4-COLOR +
MACHINE MATT SEAL
+ SPOT GLOSS UV
THROUGHOUT

UK

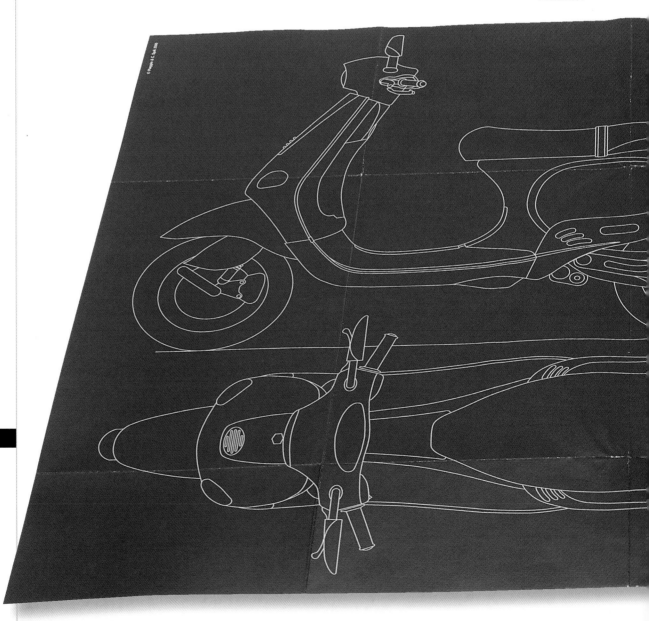

Donna Air

Jasper Conran

151
REBECCA FOSTER DESIGN
ARTVESPA

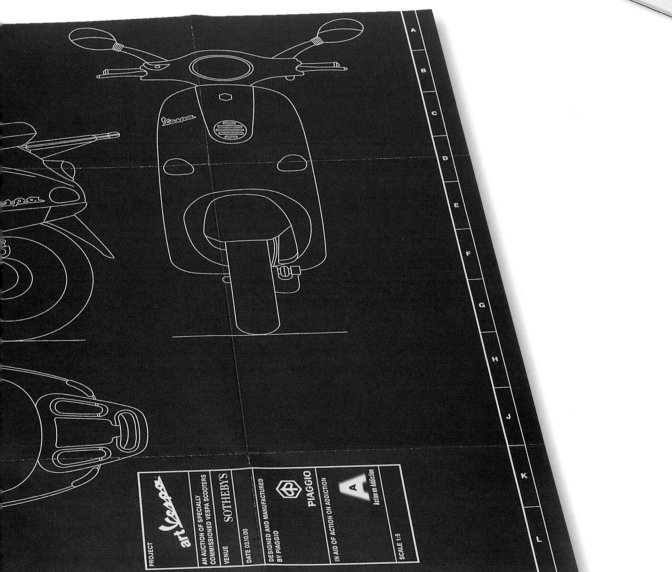

Priory Promotions present
Rab Noakes and Fraser Speirs

rupert clamp

152
BLUE RIVER DESIGN
BUDDLE ARTS GALA BROCHURE

ART DIRECTOR:
LISA THUNDERCLIFFE

DESIGNER:
LISA THUNDERCLIFFE

CLIENT:
NORTH TYNESIDE
ARTS

SOFTWARE:
PHOTOSHOP
QUARKXPRESS

MATERIALS:
300 GSM PEREGRINA
+ 150 GSM HELLO
MATT

PRINTING:
2-COLOR LITHO

No-Fi present

frank bretschneider

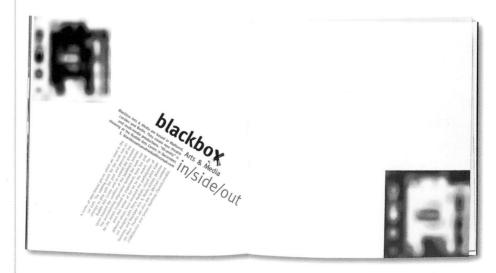

blackbox
Arts & Media
in/side/out

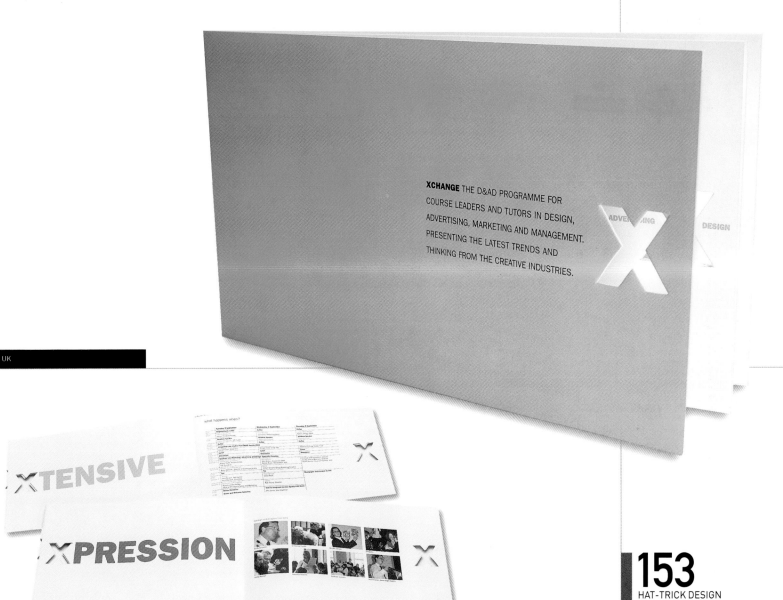

XCHANGE THE D&AD PROGRAMME FOR COURSE LEADERS AND TUTORS IN DESIGN, ADVERTISING, MARKETING AND MANAGEMENT. PRESENTING THE LATEST TRENDS AND THINKING FROM THE CREATIVE INDUSTRIES.

153
HAT-TRICK DESIGN
XCHANGE

DESIGNER:
HAT-TRICK DESIGN

CLIENT:
D&AD

SOFTWARE:
QUARKXPRESS

MATERIALS:
ESSENTIAL OFFSET

PRINTING:
LITHO & RAM-
PUNCHED

BOOKS TITLE Mennonites – Larry Towell STUDIO Atelier Works ART DIRECTION & DESIGN Quentin Newark, David Hawkins CLIENT Phaidon Press PRINTER Phaidon Press

ART DIRECTORS: CHRISTINE FENT GILMAR WENDT

DESIGNERS: CHRISTINE FENT GILMAR WENDT

CLIENT: ISTD

SOFTWARE: QUARKXPRESS

MATERIALS: CONSORT ROYAL

PRINTING: PERIVAN

154
CHRISTINE FENT + GILMAR WENDT
ISTD02 AWARDS CATALOG

ISTD 01

International Society of Typographic Designers

International TypoGraphic Awards 2001

CATALOGS TITLE Rodinsky's Whitechapel STUDIO Eggers + Diaper ART DIRECTION & DESIGN Mark Diaper CLIENT Artangel, Center van Noord PRINTER Mart Spruijt, Amsterdam

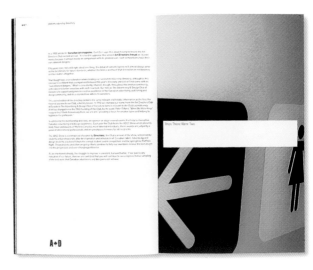

155
HAMBLY & WOOLLEY INC
2000 MEMBERSHIP DIRECTORY

ART DIRECTOR:
BARB WOOLLEY

DESIGNER:
DOMINIC AYRE

PHOTOGRAPHER:
DOMINIC AYRE

CLIENT:
ADVERTISING +
DESIGN CLUB OF
CANADA

PRINTING:
ARTHURS JONES
CLARKE

FILM

Nm.No.03

Photo: Ivan Šijak Nm.No.03

When I think about film

by Srđan Karanović

Generally speaking I dare say that film this century is still the widest, greatest, most beautiful and most universal oasis for all souls and fates incapable of adjusting to real life. As well as for those who have chosen the cinema as a vocation and those who flee only occasionally from real life by going to the cinema or, these days more frequently, dropping into the video club or changing television channels to avoid the ever-more hollow appearances of politicians and those who comment on them.

The parallel worlds of film discourse

by Goran Gocić

EUROPE. The cynic recognises feminist films easily by the fact that their creators (most of them), like their writers and their leading ladies (most of them) parade "the right to have flabby breasts", and the films themselves (again, most of them) propound the thesis that it is better for a woman to create her own misery than to leave that honour to her chosen partner.

Advice to a young director

by Srđan Dragojević

First, learn the craft, because we no longer have Communism, Stalinism, prison camps and other resources with which we managed to defeat even a Midnight Cowboy. There are none of the sexual revolutions, aristocratic shamblings and charming European amateurisms of the sixties.

Second, if we still want to lick the West's sweet, body-built, supermodel butt and hide ourselves in it, we must steel ourselves to play the creative snitch on our sad reality, add a little tasty swill from our relapse into Communism and demonstrate that there's still no democracy on the horizon here (let alone rights for gays and lesbians), to explain that our nation is scum, the asshole of the civilised world. But – and Pay Attention Now! – we're scum with wild and storm-tossed emotions which lead our heroes to death and madness and us artists to the golden oleander or some such trinkets intended for Papuan-Balkans directors. Long may we live! And a happy hundredth birthday to our film industry.

Great master

by Nadežda Milenković and Ana V

When Fellini makes a tele commercial it appears news, and not in the adver breaks before and. It's obvious that advertisers it for the money. The consu money. And that clients inve money in the pursuit consumer's buck. Ba Roma's recent campaign we in at thirty million de

Fellini's witty comment wa he had initially planned to thieves breaking into the ban finding, to their surprise, was completely empty. The over would have explained don't have any money becaus gave it all to Fellini to d comme

FILMSKI LETAK
SLOBODAN ŠIJAN • FILM LEAFLET(S)

NEW MOMENT

ADVER
TEASING

⇒

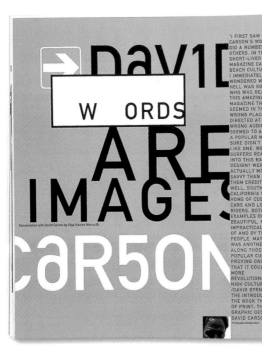

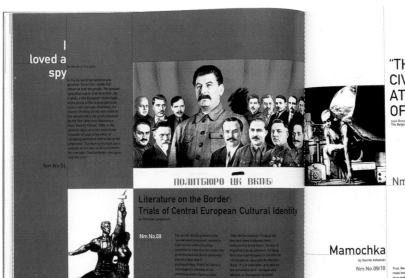

ART DIRECTORS:
EDUARD ČEHOVIN
SLAVIMIR
STODANOVIČ

DESIGNERS:
EDUARD ČEHOVIN
SLAVIMIR
STODANOVIČ

PHOTOGRAPHER:
JUGOSLAV VLAHOVIC

MATERIALS:
CHARGONET

PRINTING:
DELO PRINTING
HOUSE

ART DIRECTOR:
DENIS DULUDE

DESIGNER:
DENIS DULUDE

ILLUSTRATOR:
TOMASZ WALENTA

PHOTOGRAPHER:
POL BARIL

CLIENT:
IMPOSTOR
ENTERTAINMENT

SOFTWARE:
ILLUSTRATOR
PHOTOSHOP
QUARKXPRESS

CANADA

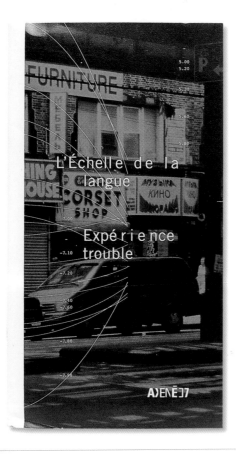

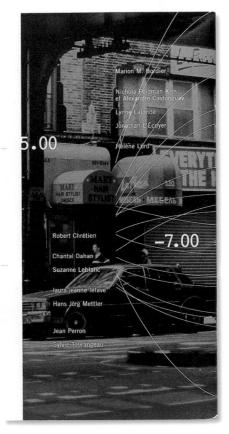

ART DIRECTOR:
MIKE TEIXEIRA

DESIGNER:
MIKE TEIXEIRA

CLIENT:
AXENÉOR/CENTRE
D'ARTISTES

PRINTING:
M.O.M. GROUP

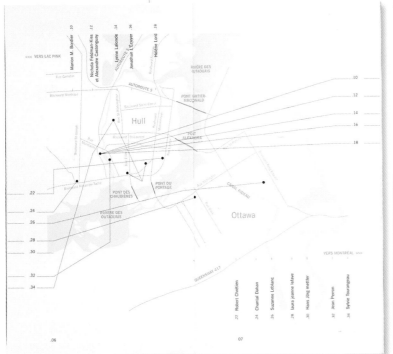

158
KOLÉGRAMDESIGN
ÉCHELLE DE LA LANGUE

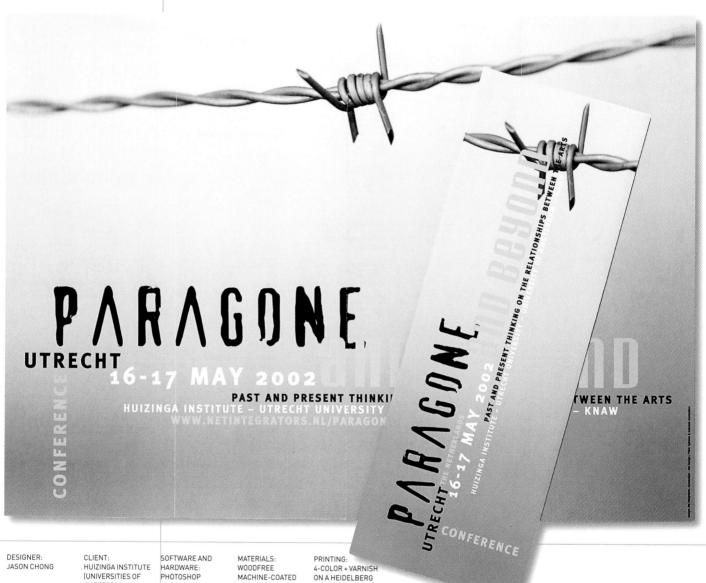

ART DIRECTOR:
JASON CHONG

DESIGNER:
JASON CHONG

CLIENT:
HUIZINGA INSTITUTE
(UNIVERSITIES OF
AMSTERDAM &
UTRECHT)

SOFTWARE AND
HARDWARE:
PHOTOSHOP
QUARKXPRESS
APPLE CUBE
PC

MATERIALS:
WOODFREE
MACHINE-COATED
170 GSM

PRINTING:
4-COLOR + VARNISH
ON A HEIDELBERG
SPEEDMASTER 72
PRESS

159
NET INTEGRATORS – NET DESIGN
CONFERENCE POSTER/FLYER/PROGRAM
(PRO BONO)

SOMMAIRE GILLES GROULX, L'INTÉGRALE | PETER KUBELKA : AUTOPORTRAITS DE L'ARTISTE | LES CHEMINS DE ROSSELLINI | ALEKSANDR PTOUCHKO | ANNE-MARIE MIÉVILLE | NOUVEAU CINÉMA TCHÈQUE | SEMAINE D'ACTIONS CONTRE LE RACISME | LA COOP VIDÉO A 25 ANS | MÉMENTO POUR HUBERT AQUIN | LARRY KENT | TOUJOURS PAGNOL | SPIRAFILM, LE 25e | PLACE AUX VARIÉTÉS | PROGRAMMES HEBDOMADAIRES DE MARS ET AVRIL 07–19 | INDEX DES CYCLES ET DES TITRES 25–27 | INFORMATIONS 28 |

MARS-AVRIL 2002

68 LA REVUE
DE LA CINÉMATHÈQUE

SOMMAIRE PRÉSENTATION 03 | JAIME HUMBERTO HERMOSILLO LA PROFONDEUR DU QUOTIDIEN SELON HERMOSILLO 05 | TOTÒ TOTÒ SUR LA RUE SAINT-LAURENT 06 | VALERIO ZURLINI LE STYLE ET LES ÉMOTIONS 08–09 | SÉRIES FRANÇAISES 15 | MONTY PYTHON 21 | AUTOBIOGRAPHIE 29 | JAZZ À L'ÉCRAN 33 | EXPOSITION ET INFORMATIONS 38 | CINÉMATOGRAPHIE 23 |

JUIN-JUILLET-AOÛT 2001

64 LA REVUE
DE LA CINÉMATHÈQUE

SOMMAIRE MERCI MONSIEUR SCORSESE | 03 | CARL TH. DREYER, CINÉASTE DE L'IRRÉMÉDIABLE 05 | L'AUTRE DOUBLE D'ALAIN ROBBE-GRILLET 05 | L'ACPAV / LE 30e 09 | L'ANIMATION D'AVANT-GARDE DU XXe SIÈCLE 12 | PREMIER PLAN 15 | TÉLÉTHÉÂTRE : CRÉATIONS ORIGINALES 18 | PROGRAMMES HEBDOMADAIRES DE JANVIER ET FÉVRIER 07–19 | INDEX DES CYCLES ET DES TITRES 23–27 | INFORMATIONS 28 | EXPOSITIONS 29 |

67 LA REVUE
DE LA CINÉMATHÈQUE

SOMMAIRE L'ANIMATION : UN DÉFI DE RIGUEUR 03 | ARTE DOCUMENTAIRES 05 | AGNIESZKA HOLLAND 05 | TRAJECTOIRE DE JEAN-DANIEL POLLET 06 | LE CINÉMA SCIENTIFIQUE FRANÇAIS 07 | GÉRARD BLAIN 14 | PIOTR SAGEPIN 18 | PROGRAMMES HEBDOMADAIRES DE NOVEMBRE ET DÉCEMBRE 07–19 | INDEX DES CYCLES ET DES TITRES 23–27 | INFORMATIONS 28 | EXPOSITIONS 29 |

NOVEMBRE-DÉCEMBRE 2001

66 LA REVUE
DE LA CINÉMATHÈQUE

ARTE
documentaires

ART DIRECTOR:
ANNIE LACHAPELLE

DESIGNER:
ANNIE LACHAPELLE

CLIENT:
CINÉMATHÈQUE
QUÉBÉCOISE

SOFTWARE:
ILLUSTRATOR
PHOTOSHOP
QUARKXPRESS

CANADA

160
KO CREATION
LA REVUE

VALERIO ZURLINI :
LE STYLE ET LES ÉMOTIONS

DANS *CRONACA FAMILIARE*, VALERIO ZURLINI A SURTOUT FILMÉ UNE VOIX, LA VOIX DE MARCELLO MASTROIANNI QUI DONNE VIE À LA CONVERSATION INTIME ENTRE UN ÉCRIVAIN (ENRICO) ET SON FRÈRE DISPARU. PLUS QU'UNE ADAPTATION CINÉMATOGRAPHIQUE LITTÉRALE DE CE TEXTE TIRÉ DU ROMAN COURT ET INTENSE DE VASCO PRATOLINI, ZURLINI A RÉELLEMENT TRADUIT CES PAROLES EN IMAGES. CE SONT CES PAROLES QUI SONT LE REFLET CACHÉ DES MAISONS ÉTROITES ET DES MURS D'UNE FLORENCE DÉSERTE COMME ON PEUT LE VOIR DANS LE CADRAGE DE OTTONE ROSAI QUI LES ONT INSPIRÉS.

ANTONIO COSTA

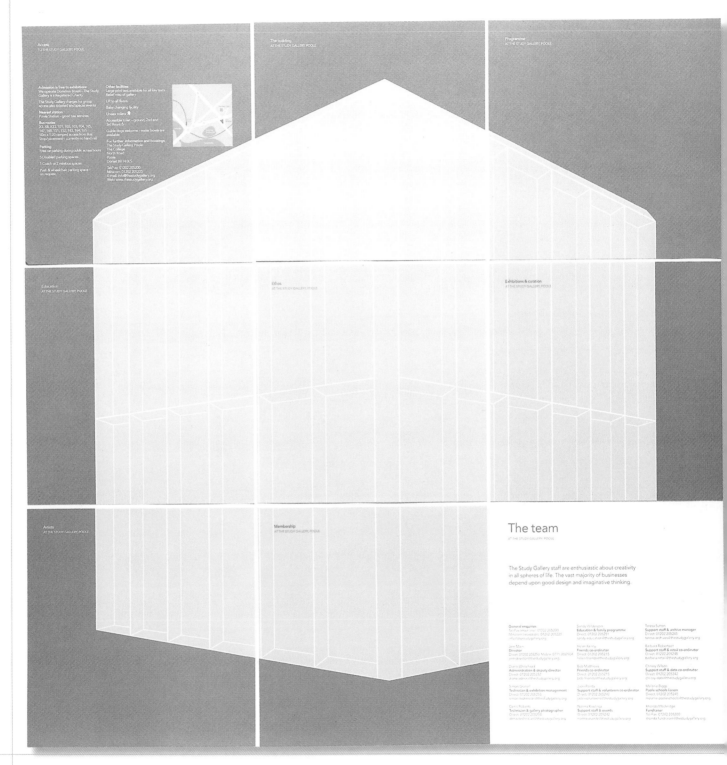

ART DIRECTORS:
RICHARD MCGILLAN
CHLOE STEERS

CLIENT:
THE STUDY GALLERY
POOLE

PRINTING:
2-COLOR LITHO

Text/Images/Sounds

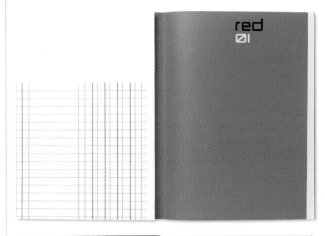

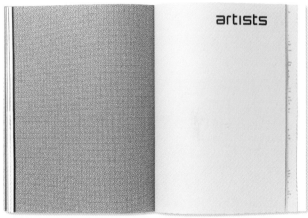

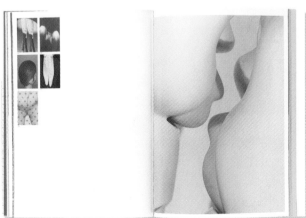

ART DIRECTOR:
FABIO ONGARATO

DESIGNER:
JAMES LIN

CLIENT:
AUSTRALIAN CENTRE
FOR CONTEMPORARY
ART

MATERIALS:
MIX OF STOCKS

PRINTING:
ENERGI

AUSTRALIA

Products for
Health & Leisure

iPod
Design Group
Apple Industrial Design
Client
Apple Computer

23
Product Design
Sponsored by
Keen

Products
for the Home

Muji CD Player
Design Group
IDEO Japan
Client
Muji

Products
for Work

Plateau
Design Group
Staverton
Client
Staverton

Titanium
PowerBook G4
Design Group
Apple Industrial Design
Client
Apple Computer

iBook
Design Group
Apple Industrial Design
Client
Apple Computer

26

24
Editorial &
Book Design
Sponsored by
Phaidon Press

Complete Books

You Can Find
Inspiration In
Everything
Design Group
Aboud.Sodano
Client
Violette Editions

American
Photography 17
Design Group
344 Design LLC
Client
Amilus

Identifying Courage
Design Group
Slaughter Hanson
Client
The Alabama Memorial
Foundation

Complete Magazines

Mined Field Issue 1/2
Design Group
Tank Publications
Client
Tank Publications

1981
Assassination
attempt on Reagan

"I SHOT HIM"
REID MILES

PHOTOGRAPHER – REID MILES / ART DIRECTOR – TONY KAYE
AGENCY – CDP / CLIENT – WHITBREAD
AGENTS: TONY McAPEL ASSOCIATES LTD. 01-240 1636 TELEX 888607.

163
NB:STUDIO
D&AD BOOK OF THE NIGHT

ART DIRECTORS:
ALAN DYE
NICK FINNEY
BEN STOTT

DESIGNER:
NICK VINCENT

CLIENT:
D&AD

SOFTWARE:
ILLUSTRATOR
QUARKXPRESS

MATERIALS:
COVER: DUFLEX
ENGRAVING
TEXT: GALLERIE SILK

PRINTING:
VENTURA

120
Future Creative
Chris Christou,
Deborah Latimer

055
FutureBrand
David Davies, Sven
Skaara, Robert Soar,
Claude Salzburger, Erik
de Graaf, Ian Scoffield,
Drew Smith, Annegro
Gulla, David Hensley,
Martin Amann, Martina
Blankenburg, Robert
Monaghan

063
FutureBrand
Charles Trevail,
Samantha Dumont,
Jan Oldenburger, Adam
Toensburg, Mark Staton,
Marcio Moreira, Peter
Stimpson, John Ellens,
Kerstin Gimmeney,
Robert Muchin, and
Guest of FutureBrand

064
FutureBrand
Christopher Nurke,
Cristina Vicedo, Alan
Rude, James Roberts,
Adlai Stock, Tim
Simmons, Francesco
Moretti, Elizabeth Finn,
Jooper von Wieding,
Guest of FutureBrand

159
Garretts
Sue Hildrey, Gerald
Berman, Nat Taylor,
Hans Elias, 8 Guests
of Garretts

123
Getty Images
Sue Farr, Franz
Prenner, John Hagelin,
Sallyanne Heywood,
Lauren Munton,
Andrew Duncomd,
Robert Gubas,
Chris Green, Andrew
Saunders, Chris
Ainsworth, 2 Guests
of Getty Images

131
Getty Images
12 Guests of
Getty Images

161
Glassworks
Zoe Rogers, Alastair
Hearsum, Sadie Ward,
Sean Elliot, Erica
Bengton, Jason Kelley,
Liz Roberts, Clare
Howell, Hector
MacLeod, Thea Slevin

045
Glenfiddich
12 Guests of
Glenfiddich

024
Godman
Jo Godman, 11 Guests
of Godman

100
Gorgeous
Peter Thwaites,
Tom Carty, David
Lindo, Paul Rothwell,
Sarah-Jane Rothwell,
Suza Horvat, Flora
Fernandez-Marengo,
Spencer Dodds,
Lucie Cooper,
1 Guest of Gorgeous

162
Graphics International
Natalie Avella, Warren
Parkinson

059
Grey Interactive/Joshua
12 Guests of Grey
Interactive/Joshua

058
Grey Odense
Ricardo Cámara, Line
Dahl, Tage Østbjerg,
Bodil Villumsen, Kim
Gørtiz, Pernille H.
Danielsen

051
Grey Worldwide
Roger Kilmartin,
Beverley Fartnum,
Kai Marks, Roger
Manton, Stephanie
Wellesley, Barry Brand,
Paul Pickengill, Sandra
Blackford, Andy
Blackford, Dee Butler,
Guest of Grey
Worldwide

life begins at 40!

**happy birthday dandad
love from all @ seymourpowell**
www.seymourpowell.com
020 7381 6433

ANNI KUAN

HAPPILY INVITES YOU IN THIS YEAR OF
THE HORSE TO THE FASHION COTERIE
TO PREVIEW THE FALL AND WINTER
2002 COLLECTION

FROM SUNDAY, FEB 24 2002 TO TUESDAY, FEB 26
2002, PIER 92, BOOTH #1638, NEW YORK CITY

REPRESENTED BY

CYNTHIA OCONNOR & COMPANY
141 WEST 36TH STREET, SUITE 12A
NEW YORK CITY, NY 10018
TEL 212·594 4999 FAX 212·594 0770

ANNI KUAN STUDIO
242 WEST 38TH STREET
11TH FLOOR
NEW YORK CITY, NY 10018
TEL 212·704 4038
FAX 212·704 0651

USA

ART DIRECTOR:
STEFAN SAGMEISTER

DESIGNER: MATHIAS
ERNSTBERGER

PHOTOGRAPHER:
MATHIAS
ERNSTBERGER

CLIENT:
ANNI KUAN DESIGN

MATERIALS:
NEWSPRINT +
PLASTIC HORSE

LINEAGE
THE ARCHITECTURE OF DANIEL LIBESKIND

165
FABIO ONGARATO DESIGN
LINEAGE: THE ARCHITECTURE OF
DANIEL LIBESKIND

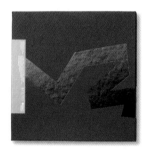

ART DIRECTOR:
FABIO ONGARATO

DESIGNER:
JAMES LIN

CLIENT:
JEWISH MUSEUM OF
AUSTRALIA

MATERIALS:
NORDSET

PRINTING:
GUNN & TAYLOR

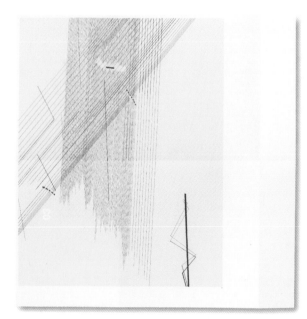

07
POINT, LIFE,
LINE

166
FABIO ONGARATO DESIGN
BRIGHT & SHINING

ART DIRECTOR:
FABIO ONGARATO

DESIGNER:
FABIO ONGARATO

CLIENT:
AUSTRALIAN
EMBASSY,
TOKYO

MATERIALS:
PARILUX

PRINTING:
ALTSHUL PRINTING

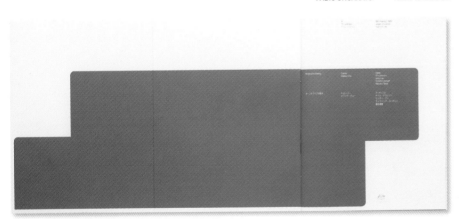

AUSTRALIA

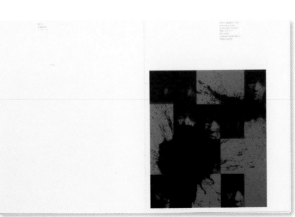

Entertaining Benefits Exclusive use of the Serpentine Gallery in June and July + Multiple entertaining opportunities + Contemporary and elegant settings + In-house Events Organisers Corporate Employee Benefits Private tours and talks + Limited edition prints for company offices + Discounts at the Serpentine Bookshop + invitations to openings + Priority booking for Serpentine Gala events Sponsorship Opportunities Exhibition sponsorship + Education Programme funding + Special Projects and Events sponsorship

167
FROST DESIGN
SERPENTINE CORPORATE BENEFACTORS

ART DIRECTOR:
VINCE FROST

DESIGNER:
VINCE FROST

CLIENT:
THE SERPENTINE
GALLERY

PRINTING:
FARRINGDON
PRINTERS (LITHO)

Man Ray, Henry Moore, Andy Warhol, Bridget Riley, Damien Hirst and Rachel Whiteread are just a few of the artists who have exhibited at the Serpentine Gallery.

"The Serpentine is a rare gallery. Its like cannot be found anywhere else in Britain, or anywhere I can think of beyond Britain." The Sunday Times

UK

168
CHIMERA DESIGN
FRUEAUF VILLAGE

FRUEAUFVILLAGE
HIGHINTHE
AUSTRALIAN
ALPS

ART DIRECTOR:
JOHN MAGART

DESIGNER:
SHELLEY BENSON
NAOMI MACE
KATHERINE CHADWICK

CLIENT:
FRUEAUF VILLAGE

SOFTWARE:
ILLUSTRATOR

MATERIALS:
RALEIGH PAPER

PRINTING:
BAMBRA PRESS
SANDERSON
COMPLETE COLOUR

You always
wanted to
drive…

RALLY SCHOOL

"Those guys on TV make it
look so easy. Believe me, it's
much tougher than it looks."
Tony Anderson, Surveyor

169
CARTER WONG TOMLIN
OCTAGON MOTORSPORTS BROCHURE

RALLY SCHOOL

The quickest way to get from A to B? Sideways.

Don't let anybody tell you that all the most exhilarating driving experiences
take place on the race track…

Scrabbling for grip. Sawing at the wheel. Sliding into one handbrake turn after another. Never pointing in a straight line. But always going forward, rapidly. With a professional rally driver as your co-driver, you'll discover how you can safely push a competition-spec Escort Cosworth or a works-built Peugeot 106 GTi to its limits. Your racing heartbeat is matched only by the constant hammering of gravel, as you battle to be quickest around our purpose-built rally stages.

Serious about rallying competitively? Then our Advanced Rally Driving Course is for you, the perfect opportunity to learn the skills that it takes to become a real rally driver and even to compete in a genuine rally in a works Peugeot 106 GTi Cup Car.

Rally School Venues
Brands Hatch
Silverstone
Oulton Park
Donington & Croft

For further information, please turn to pages 38 and 39

22 **Booking** 08705 125250 www.octagonmotorsports.com

Booking 08705 125250 www.octagonmotorsports.com 23

ART DIRECTOR:
PHIL CARTER

DESIGNER:
NEIL HEDGER

CLIENT:
OCTAGON
MOTORSPORTS

SOFTWARE AND
HARDWARE:
ILLUSTRATOR
MAC

MATERIALS:
MEGAMATT

PRINTING:
LITHO 4-COLOR +
2 SPECIALS

UK

ORANGEARROWS AX3

"The OrangeArrows AX3
has been designed to give
a truer experience than
ever before of what an F1
driver sees and feels from
the cockpit. A lot has been
written about the
acceleration, braking and
braking forces…

Sam Rowntree, Team Principal

The ultimate motorsport experience? No, much better than that.

Yes, of course, you love to drive. But, just occasionally, it's better to be a passenger.

ORANGEARROWS AX3
Silverstone

6 **Booking** 08705 125250 www.octagonmotorsports.com

Booking 08705 125250 www.octagonmotorsports.com 7

ART DIRECTOR:
DANIEL BASTIAN

DESIGNERS:
DANIEL BASTIAN
MAYA DA SILVA
JUTTA HOFFMANN

PHOTOGRAPHER:
TOM KLEINER

CLIENT:
DESIGN ZENTRUM
BREMEN

SOFTWARE:
PHOTOSHOP
QUARKXPRESS

MATERIALS:
ZANDERS MEGA
MATT 135 OFFSET

PRINTING:
FRANKE DRUCK

büro 7

gruppe für gestaltung

bremer gestalten

josef hattig

Eine Ausstellun

im Design Zent um Bremen

Das Gestaltungsbüro entwickelt und realisiert seit 1993 umfassende Kommunikationskonzepte zur Umsetzung marktgerechter Unternehmensstrategien. Auf der Basis von fundierten Analysen werden Lösungen erarbeitet, die die Unternehmensidentität des Kunden nach innen und außen effektiv kommunizieren.

Büro 7. Telefon 0421-7 37 07

14 Gestalter unterschiedlicher Fachrichtungen arbeiten in den Bereichen Werbung, Grafik, Interieurdesign und Möbelgestaltung. Diese Zusammenarbeit unterschiedlicher Disziplinen führt zu ganzheitlichen Gestaltungslösungen.

Gruppe für Gestaltung Telefon 0421-33 86 80

Mein Haus versteht Designförderung immer als Wirtschaftsförderung und auch als Hilfe zur Selbsthilfe. Sie soll sowohl die Innovationskraft von Unternehmen stärken als auch das im Bundesland Bremen vorhandene kreative Potential sichtbar machen und mehren.

Das Design Zentrum Bremen hat daher eine Ausstellungsserie begonnen, in der die Vielfalt kreativer Dienstleistungen im Designbereich am Beispiel vorwiegend kleinerer und jüngerer Designbüros gezeigt wird.

Wir hoffen, daß bereits die erste Ausstellung dieser Reihe vielen mittelständischen Unternehmen, aber auch Existenzgründern den Anstoß gibt, Design in ihre Unternehmensstrategie einzubeziehen.

Der Ausstellung, die im Rahmen von „Advantage: Design" der Design-Initiative der deutschen Wirtschaft stattfindet, wünsche ich einen großen Erfolg, zahlreiche Kontakte zwischen Unternehmern und Designern und viel öffentliche Resonanz.

Josef Hattig
Senator für Wirtschaft, Mittelstand, Technologie
und Europaangelegenheiten

GERMANY

170
FORM5 + BÜRO7
BREMERGESTALTEN

er

renate wedepohl

Schmuck zum Gernetragen. Egal ob zum Alltagskleid oder zum kleinen Schwarzen, die Kollektionen der Schmuckdesignerin verleihen jedem Outfit den letzten Schliff. Ausgewogene Proportionen und klassische Materialien bestimmen das charakteristische Erscheinungsbild ihrer Werke. Schlichtes Silber, üppiges Gold und kühles Platin stehen sich oft komplementär gegenüber und erzeugen einen spannungsreichen Kontrast zwischen strenger Geometrie und verspielten Ornamenten.

Renate Wedepohl. Telefon 0421-70 39 22

lina namuth

Seit 1984 entwirft die Künstlerin in ihrer eigenen Werkstatt Damen- und Herren-Oberbekleidung aus hochwertigen und originellen Stoffen. Jedes Stück erscheint als Unikat oder im Rahmen einer Kleinserie, was dem Kunden große Individualität garantiert. „Mein Ziel ist es, Kleidung zu entwickeln, die das Leben angenehm macht, die Patina ansetzen darf wie ein gutes Möbelstück, in der man alles tun kann." Die Mode von Lina Namuth ist schlicht, bequem, elegant und einfach zu tragen.

Lina Namuth. Telefon 0421-32 63 66

ITALY

ART DIRECTORS: DESIGNERS: CLIENT: PRINTING:
LIONELLO BOREAN   LIONELLO BOREAN   MALOFANCON   CMYK + 1 PANTONE
CHIARA GRANDESSO   CHIARA GRANDESSO   FURNITURE

5453

SOME TRAINS IN AMERICA

ART DIRECTOR:
VINCE FROST

DESIGNER:
VINCE FROST

PHOTOGRAPHER:
ANDREW CROSS

CLIENT:
CHRIST BOOT/
PRESTEL

MATERIALS:
EURO ART SILK
170GSM

PRINTING:
EBS. ITALY

0006: SOUTHERN CALIFORNIA 0030: TEXAS 0040: APPALACHIA 0062: NORTHEAST 0088: MIDWEST 0114: NORTHWEST 0140: CENTRAL CALIFORNIA

0088

SOME TRAINS IN AMERICA: MIDWEST 	IROQUOIS JCT IL 2001

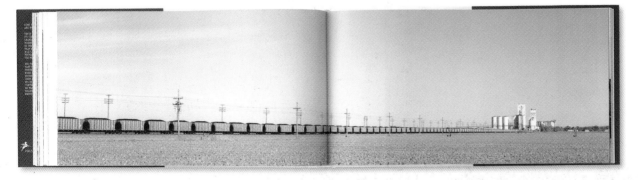

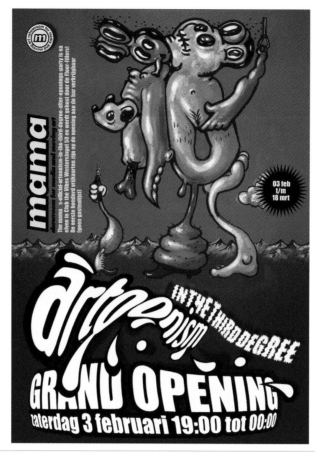

Onder de titel 'Artoonism in the third degree' presenteert showroom MAMA het werk van Luuk Bode, Cirque de Pepin, Hans van Bentem & DJ Chantelle. De derde tentoonstelling alweer in de serie 'Dutch Artoonists'. De Artoonisten bouwen hun kunstwerken op uit elementen, ontleend aan underground strips, Japanse manga en massamedia.'

ART DIRECTOR:	DESIGNER:	ILLUSTRATOR:	CLIENT:	SOFTWARE:	MATERIALS:	PRINTING:
PING-PONG DESIGN	PING-PONG DESIGN	PING-PONG DESIGN LUUK BODE CIRQUE DE PEPIN HANS VAN BENTEM DJ CHANTELLE	MAM SHOWROOM FOR MEDIA AND MOVING ART	ILLUSTRATOR PHOTOSHOP QUARKXPRESS	REVIVA OFFSET POLAR SUPER GESATINEERD	OFFSET

173
PING-PONG DESIGN
ARTOONISM

ART DIRECTOR:
FABIO ONGARATO

DESIGNER:
JAMES LIN

CLIENT:
KAREN WALKER

MATERIALS:
SILK GLOSS

PRINTING:
ENERGI

| KAREN WALKER WOMAN STOCKISTS | SANTA MONICA SHARON SEGAL 420 BROADWAY SANTA MONICA PH: 1 310 576 6062 | SYDNEY ORSON & BLAKE 83-85 QUEEN ST WOOLAHRA SYDNEY PH: 61 2 9326 1155 | WELLINGTON KAREN WALKER 126 WAKEFIELD ST CENTRAL WELLINGTON PH: 64 4 499 3558 | NEW ZEALAND KAREN WALKER PO BOX 9694 WELLESLEY ST AUCKLAND 1036 NEW ZEALAND PH: 64 9 358 0864 FAX: 64 9 358 0865 EMAIL: murray@karenwalker.com | ART DIRECTOR AND DESIGN FABIO ONG DESIGN |

175
HATCH CREATIVE
BODYTORQUE

ART DIRECTOR:
SASKIA ERICSON

DESIGNER:
SASKIA ERICSON

PHOTOGRAPHER:
LOIS GREENFIELD

CLIENT:
THE AUSTRALIAN
BALLET

SOFTWARE:
ILLUSTRATOR
PHOTOSHOP
STREAMLINE

MATERIALS:
GILCLEAR OXFORD
GILBERT PAPER

PRINTING:
4-COLOR PROCESS
BAMBRA PRESS

ART DIRECTOR:
JOHN SAYLES

DESIGNERS:
JOHN SAYLES
SOM INTHALANGSY

ILLUSTRATOR:
JOHN SAYLES

CLIENT:
AMERICAN
INSTITUTE OF
ARCHITECTS,
IOWA

SOFTWARE AND
HARDWARE:
ILLUSTRATOR
QUARKXPRESS
MAC

MATERIALS:
MOHAWK NAVAJO
WHITE, VARIOUS

PRINTING:
OFFSET

176
SAYLES GRAPHIC DESIGN
BREAKING NEW GROUND
CONFERENCE 2001

AGENCY DIRECTORY

090 **AJANS ULTRA**
ASLAN YATAGIS. FEZA AP. 33/1/12
80060 CIHANGIR
ISTANBUL 80060
TURKEY
T: 0212 243 0854
NAZLIONGAN@YAHOO.COM

046
050 **ALLEMANN ALMQUIST & JONES**
301 CHERRY STREET
THIRD FLOOR
PHILADELPHIA, PA 19106
UNITED STATES
T: 215-829-9442
JAN@AAJDESIGN.COM

013
068
100 **ATTIK**
3RD FLOOR
1 HEDDON STREET
LONDON W1B 4BD
UNITED KINGDOM
T: 020 7439 9918
JULIEM@ATTIK.COM

146 **BISQIT DESIGN**
5 THEOBALDS ROAD
LONDON WC1X 8SH
UNITED KINGDOM
T: 020 7413 3028
DAPHNE@BISQIT.CO.UK

084
092 **BLOK DESIGN**
822 RICHMOND STREET WEST
SUITE 301
TORONTO, ON M6J 1C9
CANADA
T: 416-203-0187
BLOKDESIGN@EARTHLINK.NET

152 **BLUE RIVER DESIGN**
THE FOUNDRY
FORTH BANKS OFFICES
FORTH BANKS
NEWCASTLE UPON TYNE NE1 3PA
UNITED KINGDOM
T: 0191 261 0000
INFO@BLUERIVER.CO.UK

021
123 **BOSTOCK & POLLITT**
83-84 LONG ACRE
LONDON WC2E 9NQ
UNITED KINGDOM
T: 020 7379 6709

170 **BÜRO 7**
HUMBOLDSTRASSE 64
BREMEN 28203
GERMANY
T: 49 421 73706
INFO@BURO7.DE

032
039
044
048
063 **CAHAN & ASSOCIATES**
171 SECOND STREET
5TH FLOOR
SAN FRANCISCO, CA 94105
UNITED STATES
T: 415-621-0915
SHANNONHW@CAHANASSOCI-ATES.COM

019
053
056
096
098
099 **CAMPAÑEROS**
SCHULTERBLATT 36
HAMBURG 20357
GERMANY
T: 49 407809380
MDECKELMANN@CAMPANEROS.DE

169 **CARTER WONG TOMLIN**
29 BROOK MEWS NORTH
LONDON W2 3BW
UNITED KINGDOM
T: 020 7569 0000
V.SHRIMPTON@CARTERWONGTOM-LIN.COM

114
117
126 **CHEN DESIGN ASSOCIATES**
589 HOWARD STREET
FOURTH FLOOR
SAN FRANCISCO, CA 94105
UNITED STATES
T: 415-896-5338
INFO@CHENDESIGN.COM

105
115 **CHENG DESIGN**
UNIVERSITY OF WASHINGTON
BOX 353440
ART BUILDING ROOM 102
SEATTLE, WA 98195
UNITED STATES
T: 206-685-2773
KCHENG@U.WASHINGTON.EDU

055
168 **CHIMERA DESIGN**
OFFICE 2
102 CHAPEL STREET
ST KILDA, VICTORIA 3182
AUSTRALIA
T: 613 9593 6844
NAOMI@CHIMERA.COM.AU

104 **CLARK CREATIVE GROUP**
251 RHODE ISLAND STREET #204
SAN FRANCISCO, CA 94103
UNITED STATES
T: 415-487-9500
ADMIN@CLARKCREATIVE.COM

073 **C375**
TARIK ZAFER TUNAYA SOKAK 3/6
GUMUSSUYU
ISTANBUL 80040
TURKEY
T: 90.212 249 77 09
CERUTKU@C375.COM

016
095 **DESIGN ASYLUM**
46B CLUB STREET
SINGAPORE 069423
SINGAPORE
T: 65 6324 7827
CHRIS@LUNATICSATWORK.COM

071 **DESIGN5**
7636 NORTH INGRAM 102
FRESNO, CA 93711
UNITED STATES
T: 559-432-5110
STEPH@DESIGNFIVE.COM

132 **ELFEN**
TY MEANDROS
54A BUTE STREET
CARDIFF BAY CF10 5A5
UNITED KINGDOM
T: 02920 484824
GWION@ELFEN.CO.UK

072 **EMERSON, WAJDOWICZ STUDIOS**
1123 BROADWAY
SUITE 1106
NEW YORK, NY 10010
UNITED STATES
T: 212-807-8144
INFODESIGN.EWS@AOL.COM

007
036
042
097
108 **EMERY VINCENT DESIGN**
LEVEL 1
15 FOSTER STREET
SURRY HILLS
SYDNEY NSW 2010
AUSTRALIA
T: 612 9280 4233
SHANNON.GRANT@EMERYVIN-CENTDESIGN.COM

110 **ENERGY ENERGY DESIGN**
246 BLOSSOM HILL ROAD
LOS GATOS, CA 95032
UNITED STATES
T: 408-395-5911
LESLIEG@NRGDESIGN.COM

034 **EVOLVE**
STUDIO 6
42 ORCHARD ROAD
HIGHGATE
LONDON N6 5TR
UNITED KINGDOM
T: 020 8340 9541
JH@EVOLVE-DESIGN.CO.UK

018
022
026
088
162
165
166
174 **FABIO ONGARATO DESIGN**
FIRST FLOOR
569 CHURCH STREET
RICHMOND, VICTORIA 3121
AUSTRALIA
T: 613 9421 2344
RYAN@ONGARATO.CO.AU

033
076
093
149 **FAUXPAS**
HARDTURMSTRASSE. 261
ZURICH CH 8005
SWITZERLAND
T: 00411563 8638
CONTACT@FAUXPAS.CH

010
120
131 **FORM**
47 TABERNACLE STREET
LONDON EC2A 4AA
UNITED KINGDOM
T: 020 7014 1430
PAULA@FORM.UK.COM

135 **FORMAT DESIGN**
GROSSE BRUNNENSTRASSE 63
HAMBURG 22763
GERMANY
T: 49 40 32086970
ETTLING@FORMAT-HH.COM

170 **FORM5 BREMEN**
GRAF MOLTKE STRASSE 7
BREMEN 28203
GERMANY
T: 49 421 703074
BASTIAN@FORM5.DE

054 **FOSTER DESIGN GROUP**
3 ELIOT STREET
SOUTH NATICK, MA 01760
UNITED STATES
T: 508-647-5678
WEB FOSTERDESIGN.COM

052
061
087
128
144
167
172 **FROST DESIGN**
THE GYMNASIUM
KINGS WAY PLACE
SANS WALK
LONDON EC1R 0LU
UNITED KINGDOM
T: 020 7490 7994
INFO@FROSTDESIGN.CO.UK

015
134 **GRAPHICULTURE**
322 1ST AVENUE NORTH
SUITE 500
MINNEAPOLIS, MN 55401
UNITED STATES
T: 612-339-8271
JANICE@GRAPHICULTURE.COM

091
155 **HAMBLY & WOOLLEY**
130 SPADINA AVENUE
SUITE 807
TORONTO, ON M5V 2L4
CANADA
T: 416-504-2742
BOBH@HAMBLYWOOLLEY.COM

005
011
069
142 **HAND MADE GROUP**
VIA SARTORI 16
STIA, AR 52017
ITALY
T: 39 0575 582083
INFO@HMG.IT

175 **HATCH CREATIVE**
SUITE 1
147 CHAPEL STREET
ST KILDA
MELBOURNE, VICTORIA 3182
AUSTRALIA
T: 61 3 9531 8530
SAS.E@HATCHCREATIVE.COM.AU

031
064
153 **HAT-TRICK DESIGN**
STUDIO 11
CLINK STREET STUDIOS
1 CLINK STREET
LONDON SE1
UNITED KINGDOM
T: 020 7403 7875
DAVID@HAT-TRICKDESIGN.CO.UK

066 **HEBE. WERBUNG & DESIGN**
MAGSTADTERSTRASSE 12
LEONBERG 71229
GERMANY
T: 49 7152 309-20
W+D@HEBE.DE

014
047 **HORNALL ANDERSON DESIGN WORKS**
1008 WESTERN AVENUE
SEATTLE, WA 98104
UNITED STATES
T: 206-467-5800
F: 206-467-6411
C_ARBINI@HADW.COM

001 **INTERBRAND**
RADAR STUDIO
COLDBLOWLANE
THURNHAM
MAIDSTONE
KENT ME14 3LR
UNITED KINGDOM
T: 016 2273 7722
ZOE@UNTITLED.CO.UK

094
109
112
129 **IRIDIUM, A DESIGN AGENCY**
43 ECCLES STREET
2ND FLOOR
OTTAWA, ON K1R 653
CANADA
T: 613-748-3336
F: 613-748-3372
IDEAS@IRIDIUM192.COM

130 **IRON DESIGN**
120 NORTH AURORA STREET
SUITE 5A
ITHACA, NY 14850
UNITED STATES
T: 607-275-9544
F: 607-275-0370
TODD@IRONDESIGN.COM

049 **KINETIC SINGAPORE**
2 LENG KEE ROAD THYE
HONG CENTRE
#04-03A SINGAPORE 159086
SINGAPORE
T: 65 6379 5320
F: 65 6472 5440
ROY@KINETIC.COM.SG

004
057
058
139
157
160 **KO CRÉATION**
6300 PARK AVENUE
SUITE 420
MONTREAL, QC H2V 4H8
CANADA
T: 514-278-9550
F: 514-278-7253
DULUDE@KOCREATION.COM

.07